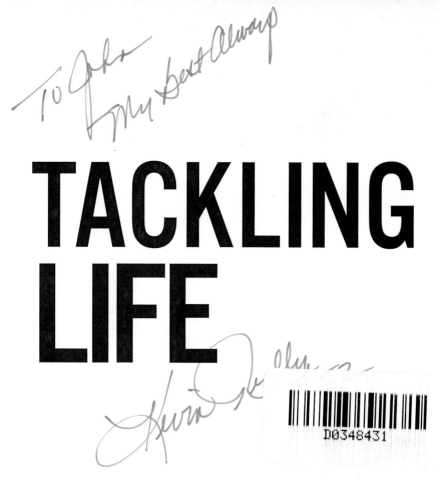

TACKLING LIFE

How Faith, Family, Friends, and Fortitude
Kept an NFL Linebacker in the Game

KEVIN REILLY

WITH JOHN RILEY

FAITH & FAMILY

PUBLICATIONS

Images courtesy of Howdy Giles and Frank Shahan.

Cover design and layout by Michael Fontecchio.

Published By:
Faith & Family Publications
PO Box 365
Downingtown, PA 19335

For more information:
www.tacklinglifebook.com
info@tacklinglifebook.com

ISBN: 978-0692960134

Printed in the United States of America

This book is dedicated to my late sister,
Karen Reilly Nardi, who defined faith and fortitude,
and Dr. Ralph Marcove, who saved my life.

Contents

Acknowledgments

This book is the story of a lifetime compiled over the past two years. Most of it is derived from my own recollection of conversations and events. Many of these are experiences that I have retold many times over the years, while others I am reliving for the first time. Sometimes, I would just sit and write for hours and days, recalling my time in the hospital or on the football field. Fortunately, I was well trained in penmanship by the nuns in grade school, so I could pass on my drafts to others for typing.

I also spent many hours and days in conversation with my friend of forty years, John Riley. Although not related, people have so often assumed we were brothers that I have stopped correcting them. John lived with me through many of my big moments, so he was able to trigger memories and help fill in details I had forgotten. His experience as a writer of local history has been invaluable. We agreed that one event would be better told by him—the time we visited Walter Reed Hospital and I addressed the amputees who had been wounded in Iraq and Afghanistan. (That story is told in Chapter 27.)

I also owe a special debt of gratitude to my daughter-in-law, Erica Reilly, who helped launch this project and has served as an editor and advisor. She helped to improve the writing and keep the book focused and on track. Erica also introduced us to Matt Pinto of Ascension Press, whose advice and contacts have been indispensable. Matt connected us to publishing consultant Mike Fontecchio and editors Patti Armstrong and Mike Flickinger, who have all been a pleasure to work with.

I have mastered a few skills with one hand, but not typing. I thank Erica and Dianna Maloy for their help in typing the manuscript.

I won't name everyone that I have bothered with phone calls to check on facts or details, but you will likely see your name in the book. Some exceptions are Ray Didinger, veteran Philadelphia sports writer and author Helene Gaillet de Neergaard. They reviewed my draft before completion and offered advice and encouragement that kept me motivated. I should also mention former Pittsburgh Steeler Rocky Bleier and Joan Kaiser, my nurse at Sloan Kettering. They helped to verify certain facts about my experiences following my amputation—a time I was under the influence of heavy medication. It was truly a special experience to reconnect with Joan after thirty-eight years.

Finally, I would like to thank my dear wife, Paula, who has served in various capacities throughout, including office administrator and chief cheerleader. Paula, I couldn't have done this without you.

Introduction

L ike many, particularly some of the veterans I have been privileged to know, my life is divided into two distinct phases—before the loss of my arm and shoulder and after. No doubt, some of the amputee combat veterans I have counseled had other events and experiences affect them both before their injury and afterwards. But I must believe that their combat exposure and traumatic injury establishes a division for them in much the same way that my amputation and long recovery has done in my life.

Many who go through such serious trauma do not always completely recover, either because the physical damage is so severe and lasting or the psychological scars are just too deep. I am convinced that my ability to have made it through the darkest days was mostly predetermined by my early physical, spiritual, and psychological development. I was blessed with wonderful parents and nurturing Catholic educators and coaches who taught me how to compete and how to win or accept defeat without losing perspective.

In Part I of my story, I weave together my early development up to achieving my dream of playing for the Philadelphia Eagles in the National Football League. As this dream of a lifetime was unfolding, however, there was a demon growing inside of me—a rare tumor that would either dramatically alter my body or take my life. I hope you will gain a sense of how each stage of my development helped to prepare me in some way for what I was facing.

In Part II, I share how the rest of my life unfolded after my four surgeries and the loss of my arm, shoulder, four ribs, and more.

This book is a story about achieving my dream, having it crushed, and then creating a new dream. The critical ingredients of my survival were faith, family, friends, and fortitude. Everyone has something they must survive, so I share my journey in hopes of encouraging others along the way.

PART I

From the Highest High to the Lowest Low

CHAPTER 1

Dreams Interrupted

New York, August 18, 1978

"Kevin, you have a desmoid tumor, and we will be lucky if I can save your arm!"

According to WebMD, desmoid tumors commonly develop in the fibrous (connective) tissue of the body that forms tendons and ligaments, usually in the arms, legs, or midsection, and also in the head and neck. These tumors look like dense scar tissue, and just like scar tissue, they adhere tenaciously to surrounding structures and organs, and, thus they are commonly difficult to remove. Surgery has been the traditional main mode of therapy for desmoid tumors, but up to 20–50% of these tumors recur after surgery.

My wife, Cathy, and I sat in a waiting room at Sloan Kettering Hospital on the Upper East Side of Manhattan. We were there to see one of the top orthopedic oncologists in the country.

The three-hour trip from my home in Wilmington, Delaware to the congested and hectic city had been exhausting. It was 11:30 AM. My appointment was supposed to be at 10:30. There were no windows and not enough seats for everyone waiting. Each passing minute increased my frustration and impatience. I selfishly regretted giving up my seat an hour earlier to a mother of a child with cancer.

Leaning against the wall and sweating profusely (a common occurrence for me, even under optimum conditions), I wiped my forehead and approached the receptionist at the front counter and asked, "How much longer do you think it will be?"

Looking up, she covered the phone with her hand. "Be patient!" she said, not very politely. "The doctor will be with you shortly."

I went back to holding up the wall while my anxiety spiked even further as I surveyed the room. There were a dozen cancer patients in varying degrees of the disease and recovery.

One patient grabbed my attention like a magnet—a little Amish boy with his parents who looked to be about six years old. Disease had ravaged his body, and he sat slumped in a folding stroller, looking more like a three- or four-year-old. He was missing his right leg below the knee, and when he slowly moved his arm to remove his Amish hat, his head was totally bald. While his parents checked their little son in, he was right in front of me and looked up. His skin was ghost white and his eyes were hollow. I smiled as our eyes met. He weakly smiled back. My stomach pitched at this brief encounter as I suddenly heard my name called.

Cathy and I were escorted into Dr. Ralph Marcove's office since all the available waiting rooms were filled. Another twenty minutes passed. Sweat dripped down my arms.

This journey had begun two years earlier on the beach in Stone Harbor, New Jersey where my parents owned a summer home. While talking sports that Memorial Day weekend with my dad, he casually asked, "What's that bump on your shoulder?"

Without a shirt in the bright sunlight, a small lump between my shoulder and my left pectorals was apparent. "Oh, this thing here? I think it's a popped muscle or something. I really notice it when I'm doing curls in the mirror. It seems to move with each rep. It's probably nothing."

My dad didn't shrug it off. "I'd get that thing looked at soon," he said. "You never know." This would turn out to be the understatement of the year.

By the time I arrived in New York, I had seen nine doctors in Wilmington and Philadelphia and had undergone two surgeries to remove the tennis ball size tumor. No one could determine why it had returned so quickly. Tests showed no signs of malignancy, but the doctors had never seen anything like it.

Dr. Ralph Marcove finally entered the room and shook my hand. He looked about fifty, 5'4" and about 150 lbs., with a full head of hair and glasses. He had the bedside manner of Sgt. Friday from the 1960s television series *Dragnet* ("Just the facts, ma'am").

While looking at the x-rays, Dr. Marcove had me take off my shirt. He grabbed my left shoulder while firmly placing his right thumb on the now protruding tumor. He pressed it real hard several times, almost bringing me to my knees as the pain fired down the left side and arm. He read the diagnosis on my chart: "benign nodular faciitis."

"That is an incorrect diagnosis," he stated looking me straight in the eye. "You have a desmoid tumor, and we will be lucky if I can save your arm. At the least you are going to probably lose your clavicle, as I predict it's attached to the tumor."

My knees buckled. Cathy and I looked at each other, stunned. It was month nine on the journey to get the tumor removed and eradicated so I could get back into in shape and resume my NFL career. Losing my left arm was never a consideration. *He's got to be kidding me*, I thought.

Before I could even catch my breath, Dr. Marcove continued. He explained that he had treated more than a hundred desmoid patients in his career. (I would soon learn he was the leading expert in the country on this rare disease.) Although desmoid tumors do not metastasize, he explained that they can be life-altering and ultimately fatal. An MRI would be scheduled, and I was to call back the following week to schedule surgery.

The entire visit lasted less than ten minutes, but it shook me like a heavyweight punch to the gut. Only two years prior I was living out my dream of playing professional football, and now I faced the prospect of being an amputee … or worse!

Still in shock from this abrupt diagnosis, I went out to the receptionist area to schedule my MRI for the following week. I noticed the little Amish boy being pushed by his parents out of the examination room.

Suddenly, Dr. Marcove reappeared at my side. "Cancel the boy's surgery for tomorrow, there is nothing else I can do for him," he said to the nurse scheduling my MRI. He said it so casually that he could just as well have been giving her his lunch order.

I was sick to my stomach. When I had gotten up that morning, I never imagined that I would be facing a world of rare tumors and amputations. Hell, I didn't even know what an MRI was. My mind raced and sweat poured off me as Cathy and I stepped outside into the blazing heat of 72nd Street.

My day had begun hoping to schedule a minor surgery so I could quickly get into shape and be on stand-by to re-enter the NFL. September was the time the injury list grew long and teams would be in the market for a special teams' player or back-up linebacker. A comeback was suddenly out of the question. Instead, I faced the possibility of losing my left arm.

How did I go from being an NFL linebacker to a potential amputee in just six hours? Badly shaken, I needed to somehow wrap my head around this whole new situation. "Let's get going," I told Cathy. "I need a beer—real bad!"

Little did I know that things were about to get much worse. Despite being operated on by one of the top orthopedic oncologists in the world and a leading expert on desmoid tumors, my surgery would render my left arm useless and leave me in excruciating pain. Only months after that surgery, the tumor would return more aggressively than ever and the race would be on to save my life.

||||||||||||||||||||||||||||||||||||||||||||||||||||||||||||||||||||||||||||||||||||||||||||||||||

CHAPTER 2

Big League Dreams

Wilmington, Delaware, during the 1950s and '60s

"You can get up now, Taylor, the game is over!"

Growing up in the suburbs in the late 1950s and early 1960s may have been the most wonderful time for adolescents in America's history. By all accounts, middle America was doing well, with the "Greatest Generation" home from World War II, starting young families and building their dream homes, and most importantly, working. After also serving in the armed forces or helping staff the war factories, many mothers were now stay-at-home moms, tending to the needs of their children. You knew everyone on your block and most of the neighbors in your immediate community.

I did not understand it at the time, but the Reilly family was

Reilly family, Christmas, 1957
Kevin Reilly, fourth grade

on the leading edge of the great suburban migration taking root after the war. Fueled nationally by a strong economy, families were leaving the cities to build or buy their dream homes on rapidly disappearing farmland. This would be a society literally driven by the automobile. The family car allowed for a new freedom of movement, and the explosion of suburban homes and automobiles became the chief drivers of the economy.

On the local level, the northern suburbs of Wilmington, Delaware, where I grew up were mostly an outgrowth of great new wealth created by one company, DuPont, and its early twentieth-century spinoffs, Hercules and Atlas. Formerly powder companies and major suppliers of the "Arsenal for Democracy," they had evolved into modern chemical companies making the products that went into the products that built the cars and homes during the great postwar economic expansion. Based on the success of revolutionary inventions such as Nylon, Dacron, Orlon, Neoprene, and Teflon, these companies funded the development of research campuses that resembled small cities and their recruiters searched the globe to find the smartest people in the world to bring them to Wilmington.

It seemed like every neighbor on your block in the '50s and '60s had a PhD, or at least a master's degree in chemical engineering. These bright minds would help create one of the outstanding public school systems in the country. They would also provide intellectual talent to a robust local private school system and the parochial school that I attended. They became the customers of all the small businesses taking root in the northern suburbs, including my father's neighborhood liquor store.

The center of much of the social and cultural life at that time was the church. For Catholics like the Reilly's, it was St. Mary Magdalen Church and School, where I received my first eight years of education. It would be hard to overstate the impact this institution and so many like it had on life at the time. The families built the church and school with their donations in the Sunday collection basket. Our pastor, Father Miller, knew everyone and truly functioned as a shepherd over his flock. While we all had our sins, the love of God, personal discipline, and respect for others were pervasive in our life and community.

I was the oldest of six children, followed by my sisters Karen and Patty, brother Sean, and sisters Kerry and Megan. My father was a WWII Navy veteran who saw service on a destroyer in the North Atlantic during the latter stages of the war. After his discharge, he became a mailman for six years before becoming part owner of a community liquor store a block from our house.

I also had a "larger than life" paternal grandfather. John E. Reilly was a prominent state senator who represented one of the toughest parts of Wilmington. He was a bit of a local philosopher, and I still find myself using quotes I learned from him as a child. Personal favorites include: "Never wrestle with a pig, the pig will like it and you'll get dirty," and "Let 'em go to hell their own way and they won't bitch going!" In 1982, an old drawbridge crossing the Christina River at the southern end of Wilmington was named in his honor.

My beautiful and popular mother possessed leadership skills that could have gone far in today's world. She was our rock and seemed always successful in rectifying any small

State Senator John E. Reilly
with President Truman, circa 1951

or large injustice that happened to us—or any kid she knew, for that matter. My mother was also a bully's worst nightmare!

Everyone played outside all the time if the weather allowed, even in the winter. On a typical summer day, after downing a bowl of cereal, you went out to play, came back home for lunch, went out to play again, back for dinner, then out again until the street lights came on. At that point, you knew you better high tail it back home. To have a parent come looking for you after dark was usually met with a slap on the back of the head or harsh words, plus the likely punishment of an earlier curfew the following evening.

Back then, there were no cell phones to check on you during the day, yet everyone felt safe. Neighborhood justice meant that other mothers had the authority to reprimand you and call your parents to report serious problems.

On an average summer day, I would eat a bowl of cereal, check the Philadelphia Phillies box score and the major league baseball standings in the newspaper, grab my baseball bat and glove and go knocking on my friends' doors to get up a sandlot game at the local park. Afternoons were spent swimming at the nearby pool or maybe building a dam in the creek that ran through the park.

When I had time alone, I would grab a basketball, baseball, or football and go into my backyard and pretend. With my fertile imagination, I saw myself as a Philadelphia Phillie, a Philadelphia Warrior (or later a 76er), or a Philadelphia Eagle, while self-broadcasting an imaginary game-changing or game-winning moment in the voice of legendary Philadelphia announcers like Bill Campbell, By Saam, or Les Keiter.

Pretending was my way of dreaming that one day I could be a Philadelphia professional athlete and that someday, I would hear the hometown fans cheer for me and the Philly team of my dreams. But it became more than a dream—it became an obsession and a passion that I would pursue at any sacrifice.

In 1962, my father acquired six Eagles season tickets courtesy of Van's Liquors, the store that he managed as co-owner along with my uncle and godfather, Bill Vandenbraak. Uncle Bill was a very successful businessman; he also owned a Chevy dealership in New Castle, Delaware. He and my dad, along with four other uncles (Bayard, Jerry, Jimmy Vandenbraak, and Jack Reilly) were the usual crew that met at the liquor store at 11:00 AM, Sunday mornings for the forty-five-minute drive to Franklin Field to see the Eagles home games.

In 1960, the Eagles won the NFL Championship, beating Vince Lombardi's Green Bay Packers in an NFL thriller that was decided by the last play of the game. Before a sellout crowd of 67,000 fans at Franklin Field, the game went back and forth with the Eagles leading 17-13. In the final minute, Packer quarterback Bart Starr spearheaded a drive to the Eagles 22-yard line with only seconds left on the clock.

Starr called the next play at the line of scrimmage and threw a slot pass to the hard-running Packer fullback Jim Taylor. Legendary Eagle tough-guy, Hall of Fame middle linebacker Chuck Bednarik was the last man between Taylor and the end zone. He crushed Taylor at the ten-yard line with a vicious tackle, pinning him to the turf as the seconds ticked off the clock, 9... 8... 7... 6... Known as "Concrete Charlie," Bednarik ensured that the Packers would not be able to run another play. With no time left, Bednarik growled at Taylor, "You can get up now. Taylor. The game is over!"

After the success and excitement of the championship season, Philadelphia's hopes ran high in the region as the 1961–62 Eagles began their quest for another NFL championship.

I was eleven years old and a huge fan of the Eagles and the Phillies. As an altar boy, I always volunteered for early Sunday Mass in the fall so I would be available in case one of the family regular ticket holders couldn't make the game. If an uncle failed to show up by 10:55, I was eligible to come off the bench and join the adults for the trip to Franklin Field.

When I got the call, I would jump on my bike and race 300 yards from our house to the store and jump into the "way back" seat of dad's 1961 Chevy station wagon. We would be off by 11:01, heading up the Industrial Highway with four uncles puffing on cigarettes and downing beers while talking nothing but Eagles football.

Franklin Field was a unique environment in those days. Seating in the stadium was on wooden benches, which made for a space challenge when winter came and topcoats were worn. After the National Anthem, season ticket holders rushed to hit the bench in musical chairs fashion, leaving the unaccustomed ticket holder with no place to fit in. Eventually, everyone squeezed in and it became a very "cozy" arrangement.

Another special element at those games was that the same people attended week in and week out. After a while, fans grew to know each other in a family-like atmosphere. Kids grew up right before your eyes, and older Eagles fans passed on their tickets to younger family members. It was, without a doubt, one of the greatest fan experiences that I ever had. Although they were not exactly comfy, there wasn't a bad seat in the house.

My favorite players at the time were Sonny Jurgensen, Tommy McDonald, and Pete Retzlaff. I idolized these players and tried to model myself after number 44, Retzlaff, a solid all-around receiver who became a local sportscaster after his playing days. All were standouts, able to score on any play. You knew that if Jurgensen, McDonald, and Retzlaff were on the field, the Eagles were rarely out of a game.

Like lots of local kids who loved sports, I often imagined myself a Philadelphia Eagle. Throwing the ball around in the yard, I would mimic Eagles announcer Bill Campbell breathlessly describing how the local player from Wilmington, Delaware saved the game with a last minute amazing touchdown catch. It was more than pretending for me, I was dreaming that someday, just maybe, if I worked hard enough, I could wear that Philadelphia Eagle uniform.

One day in 1963, my Dad and Uncle Jack announced they were going to take my brother Sean and me to see the Eagles training camp in Hershey, Pennsylvania. Uncle Jack, who was single, also happened to live next door to us and was the regular host for Eagles games on television where the adults would consume their Ballantine beer. It was in his home and on the trips to Franklin Field where the male-bonding, Eagles love fest took root in my life.

The trip to Hershey was to be a new experience and would give me the chance to meet my heroes face to face. When the day arrived, Sean and I set out determined to secure the autographs of our two favorite players, future Hall of Famers, quarterback Sonny Jurgensen and receiver Tommy McDonald.

One of the smallest receivers in the league at 165 lbs., McDonald was a big fan favorite due to his gritty style of play—always bouncing up like a Jack-in-the-box no matter how hard he was hit. Jurgensen and McDonald were becoming the league's top long ball combination and had already connected on some spectacular plays that excited the fans.

Following the two-hour drive from Wilmington, we arrived at the Hershey training camp. Conditioned to the electric atmosphere of Franklin Field, we were surprised by the thin crowds and laid-back atmosphere at camp.

Sean and I staked out the exit from the Eagles locker room with pen and paper in hand and anxiously awaited the appearance of McDonald and Jurgensen. Almost immediately, McDonald bounced out the door. I could hardly believe my eyes! Sean didn't miss a beat and blurted out, "Tommy, can I please have your autograph?"

The upbeat Eagle receiver responded, "Sure can, partner!"

I fell in right behind Sean, and at 5'10" I was looking him right in the eye. Before I could say anything, McDonald asked if I played football. "Yes sir, just like you," I squeaked out. He didn't even crack a smile—just popped his helmet on his head and sprinted onto the field.

With one down and one to go, we looked up to see the last player file out. Jurgensen must have blown right past us while we were preoccupied with all our McDonald drama. Scanning the field, I had my first Sonny Jurgensen sighting. He was lying on his back relaxing away from the other players.

A little intimidated, I took a deep breath and approached the star quarterback. He stared up at me with a toothpick in his mouth. A second later, I had his autograph. In all of five minutes, we had accomplished our mission!

McDonald and Jurgensen were now elevated above "favorite player" status. They were my heroes and I would root for them in the years ahead like they were family. Hershey and those autographs would always be our connection.

Only ten short years and 100 pounds later, I would find myself as a rookie linebacker and special team player for my beloved Eagles. Early in the 1973 season, we played the Washington Redskins at Veterans Stadium. Late in the fourth quarter, my friend and fellow linebacker Steve Zabel tore his Achilles tendon and was dispatched to the hospital by helicopter. At halftime, they told me I was going in to replace Steve, so I immediately began to refresh my mind with the defensive game plan and my specific responsibilities to defend against Redskins' quarterback Billy Kilmer.

As the game progressed, things seemed to be going well. I was so deep in concentration that I did not notice Kilmer had been injured and was taken out of the game at the end of the third quarter. When we came back to start the fourth quarter, the Redskins broke the huddle and I found myself staring in disbelief at the new quarterback—my childhood hero, Sonny Jurgensen!

At that point in his Hall of Fame career, the thirty-nine-year-old had reached nearly legendary status. And there he was, right in front of me sporting a pot belly, but with the eyes of a gunslinger. I felt like I was having an out-of-body experience!

I fought to compose myself and get ready for the snap. Jurgensen barked out, "Blue 34, blue 34, hut 1, hut 2!"

It was almost dreamlike—a slow-motion replay. I was playing against my football hero as a Philadelphia Eagle in a real NFL game.

I felt like I didn't belong on the same field with this guy and thought, *Bet he knows where I'm going on every snap of the ball.* Even the Vet Stadium fans didn't know who to root for as Jurgensen, one of the greatest pure passers the game has ever known, moved the Skins forward with three straight first downs. Fortunately, our defense collected itself (although I'm not sure

I ever did), and we held them to a field goal. Feeling personally more confident and composed during the balance of the game, our team hung on to beat Jurgensen and the Redskins.

|||||||||||||||||||||||||||||||||||||||||||||||||||||||||||||||||||||||||||||||||||||||

CHAPTER 3

The Battle to Save My Arm

New York, 1979

"Doc, it's back. The tumor is back."

Following my visit to Dr. Ralph Marcove's office, my tissue samples were sent from Temple University Hospital to Sloan Kettering. Just as Marcove predicted, under the advanced analysis available at Sloan, the diagnosis of desmoid tumor was confirmed. The doc was relatively sure he could save my arm with an operation called the Tikoff-Linberg Procedure—an operation he had performed more than a hundred times.

In layman's terms, they were going to remove my clavicle (collarbone) and scapula (shoulder blade), to which the tumor was attached, and shorten my arm by two inches between the elbow and the shoulder. Unfortunately, I would be left with no strength or lifting capability from my shoulder to the elbow, but I would be able to bend my elbow half way and retain the use of a weakened left hand. I could expect approximately fifty percent of the pre-surgery use of my arm. This would turn out to be an overly optimistic projection.

The good news, of course, was that I would most likely avoid amputation. The bad news was there would be no future in football. But I was comforted by the fact that Marcove had been successful with ninety-five percent of these surgeries. And since it was the third go at this tumor, counting the two previous operations at Temple University in Philadelphia, I hoped the third time might be the charm. After a final CT scan and blood work, it was time for Marcove to work his magic and remove the demon from my body. The operation lasted a couple of hours— much longer than he anticipated. I was out of intensive care after just one day.

On the first day back in my hospital room, Marcove arrived with a group of interns tagging after him. He explained that the tumor was about fifty percent larger than they had anticipated and was not only attached to my shoulder blade, but also lodged into my shoulder socket.

"The surgery went well, but it was more complex than I thought," Marcove explained. "We had to do more cutting than expected, so you're going to be very sore for a few weeks."

For the first time, I sensed a "chink" in the doc's armor. He was not sounding like the confident, "leading desmoid tumor expert" I had come to trust.

If the operation was supposed to reduce and eventually eliminate the pain, this was definitely not happening in the initial days following surgery. I was reassured over and over that the pain would subside as the healing continued but also cautioned that it was major surgery so my level of pain was to be expected.

I didn't know what to think, but I swallowed over-the-counter pain relievers like candy while trying to hold out on my prescription stuff for bedtime. Unfortunately, nothing worked, and I was getting four to five hours of sleep at night at most.

A week after the surgery, I decided to go out for some February fresh air and stepped on black ice in the driveway. Down I went, landing directly on the wounded shoulder. I almost passed out as the flash of pain sheared through my upper body like an electrical shock. I have often wondered if the fall triggered a regrowth of the tumor, but that is something I will never know for sure.

When I went back to my sales job at Xerox in March, I tried to do everything that I had done before the operation, but I had significant limitations since I could not raise my arm above mid chest. My arm actually got in the way when I tried to play golf or swim, so I had to strap it to my body when I jogged or it would slap against me. Having no control of it above my elbow, one very windy day at the shore a gust blew my arm up behind my back as I tried to walk down the beach.

Some lessons you just have to learn the hard way, however. A week or two after returning to work, I traveled to a customer appointment at the Getty Oil Delaware City refinery. In order to avoid the delay caused by taking my car through the gate security and the sign-in procedures, I decided to pull off the two-lane road that fronted the administrative office.

After my appointment, I returned to the car and settled in behind the wheel. My 1978 two-door Chevy Monte Carlo had very heavy doors, and I had increased the weight by pulling onto a slope with my right wheel. At this point, I had already adapted to reaching across my body with my right arm to grab the door handle to close my door.

Due to the slope, I mistakenly gripped the top of the window. I pulled up hard because of the angle and weight and caught my hand in the door. Fortunately, there was no metal frame on the window of the two-door model and there was some rubber cushion at the top to soften the impact. But I was trapped with my fingers caught in the door and my left arm completely useless.

With cars whizzing by on Route 9 and no way to communicate my plight, my mind raced as I tried to come up with a way to free myself. Fortunately, I had not yet learned the trick of tying my shoes so I was wearing loafers. I worked off my right shoe and twisted my leg up onto my lap. Twisting and wiggling, I finally reached the door handle and opened it with my toes, freeing my hand. Years later, I laugh when I tell this story, but I can assure you, it was no laughing matter at the time.

Later that summer, the pain grew even worse. I was swallowing twelve to fifteen aspirin a day and downing an entire bottle of wine before bedtime to knock myself out so I could get some sleep. Of course, I was no fun to be around, and it was taking a toll on everyone.

I struggled every day to go to work and keep up around the house, but I found myself falling behind more and more. I remained in denial that the tumor might be back and continued to hope that the pain was still a part of the healing process and a sign that better days were just around the corner.

I finally hit a wall on a cold October day at a Villanova–Delaware football game with my family. I had saved two pain pills for the homecoming weekend so I could try to enjoy the day with everyone, but the pills barely made a dent in my throbbing left shoulder. On top of the two opioids, I tried to drown things out with half a dozen beers or more.

The combination of pain, drugs, and alcohol had me acting like a college sophomore on St. Patrick's Day. It resulted in a serious man-to-man discussion with my father when we arrived home that night. "What the hell was that performance today about?" he raised his voice in frustration. "You were embarrassing, out of control, and making a fool out of yourself. You nearly started a fight in the tailgate parking lot!"

At that point, both the meds and alcohol were wearing off, and I could feel the pain beginning to build back up with my arm going numb again. I was broken, defeated, depressed, and out of answers. I started to sob. "Dad, I cannot keep going on like this." I said. "I am in constant pain, I can't sleep and I am completely worn out. I surrender!"

"OK, we are going to see Dr. Marcove first thing Monday morning," he said.

When I told him Marcove did not see patients on Mondays, he interrupted. "Kevin, we will see him Monday before he goes into surgery—I promise you."

Somehow my dad made the appointment. At 5:30 on Monday morning, we left Wilmington headed for Sloan Kettering in Manhattan. Marcove had agreed to meet us at 8:15 before he went into surgery. As we traveled north on the New Jersey Turnpike with farmland and factories appearing in the morning mist, I had a sense of relief knowing that we were headed towards a solution.

We arrived at Dr. Marcove's office at 7:30, and it was eerie to see the waiting room completely empty. At 7:45, the doctor arrived, accompanied by a young woman, a medical intern. The four of us moved to the examination room. "OK, what's the problem here?" Marcove wanted to know.

"Doc, it's back. The tumor is back."

"How do you know it's back?" His voice seemed almost condescending.

"Feel this under my armpit." For the last three weeks, I had felt a hard, small mass the size of a large marble. It was growing larger each day. It was now the size of a racquetball. I had been in a state of denial, hoping it was not desmoid, but rather normal scar tissue.

As I raised my arm, the protruding tumor was easily visible. Dr. Marcove made only a ten-second exam with his hand while everyone, including me, held our breath. He then looked me straight in the eye and said, "I'm going to have to be aggressive and get better margins this time. We're going to have to do a four-quarter amputation to be certain to get it all. It will involve amputating your left arm, left shoulder and removing four ribs."

I guess I was already resigned to this plight and asked, "When can you do it?" At about this point, the young intern turned white and dropped into a nearby chair. But I was ready. I had been suffering for months and had reached my limit. I was physically and mentally drained. The doc gave me a prescription for some serious sleep medication and told me to rest up. The surgery would take place the following Monday.

On the way home, my dad and I discussed the turn of events in my life. I was surprisingly relieved. As radical as it all sounded, at least this was a plan. It was the only alternative to beat this beast. I had the best doctor in the world handling my case, I was otherwise young and strong, and most importantly, I had a deep faith in God. I was ready and I truly felt at peace.

||||||||||||||||||||||||||||||||||||||||||||||||||||||||||||||||||||||||||||||||

CHAPTER 4

The Early High School Years – Salesianum

Wilmington, Delaware, during the 1960s

"I have taken hold and will not let go."

In response to Salesianum School winning its second straight state basketball championship in March 2015, Dave Frederick, a writer for Delaware's *Cape Gazette* wrote a column entitled "146 Reasons to Hate Salesianum." The 146 reasons are the state championships the Sals had won over the years. These wins include incredible dominance in sports such as swimming, soccer, and cross country, but it is with football that the athletic legacy of Salesianum was born. The banners hanging from the gymnasium walls cannot fully tell the story of a program so dominant that they could rarely find a local Delaware school willing to play them.

Salesianum was founded by the Oblates of St. Francis de Sales in Wilmington, Delaware in 1903. The Oblates (from the Latin *oblatus*, "someone who has been offered") were founded in 1875 by Father Louis Brisson in honor of St. Francis de Sales, a man renowned as the "Gentleman Saint" for his patience and gentleness. Francis served as Bishop of Geneva in the early seventeenth century. In his book *Introduction to the Devout Life*, he counseled charity over penance as the path to living a spiritual life.

Since its founding in 1903, the young men of Salesianum have stood out in the community, attired in their trademark coat and tie. Graduates of this iconic institution have gone on to distinguish themselves in the fields of religion, medicine, science, business, politics, sports, and military leadership. In recent years, grads have served as mayors, chiefs of police and fire, heads of the National Guard, even as the top commander of the Navy SEALS. Wherever one sees the Salesianum name, they may notice the school motto, *Tenui Nec Dimittan* ("I have taken hold and will not let go").

To understand the history and the success of this extraordinary institution, you need to learn about the men who devoted their lives to the boys who grow to become "Salesian Gentlemen." If you walk down the main hall of the school today, you will notice a display case with photos of priests and coaches who embody the legacy of "Sallies." Coaches Dominick "Dim" Montero and Father James "Buzz" O'Neill built the legendary football program and sent many young athletes on to star in some of the leading college programs around the country. And before *Brown vs. Board of Education*, Father John Birkenhauer is remembered for stepping forward to schedule a game with the all-black Howard High School in segregated Wilmington.

When Salesianum alumni gather decades later at sports events, graduations for their sons, or memorial services, they talk about the funny or dramatic moments on the athletic fields and classrooms, and, more often, about the special influence of these men on their lives. In a time when many bright and talented Wilmington kids rarely thought about college, priests like Father Robert Kenny and Father Robert Ashenbrenner helped them understand the possibilities. They continued to stay in touch with their students through college or the military, and often officiated at their weddings and baptize their children.

Those of us who attended Wilmington parochial schools in the early 1960s soon heard about the exploits of Sallies stars like Mulvena, Allen, Hall, Scott, and Alexander. Like the legendary coach Dim Montero, these football names loomed as large as the stars of the Philadelphia Eagles. And if you were a kid like me, who wanted to play football in high school, you wondered if you could ever play for the mighty Sals.

As an altar boy from sixth through eighth grades, I often saw Coach Montero at 6:30 AM Mass. A quiet and humble guy, I was to learn that he had sustained a serious head injury during combat in World War II and had a metal plate in his head. Considered a football genius, his graduating players were recruited by the top football schools in the country, including Notre Dame, Minnesota, Delaware, and Maryland.

Coach Montero spoke at our eighth-grade graduation banquet and singled me out in his remarks, saying he wanted me to come to Sallies and play football for him. I was hooked! Also, it didn't hurt that a couple of my grade school football teammates, Larry Pietropaulo and Tony Nerlinger, were headed to Sallies.

Freshmen year at Sallies was a big transition for me. I went from being a big fish in the eighth-grade pond, to a class of 259 students, many of whom were solid athletes coming out of the Catholic Youth Organization (CYO) programs. We had approximately sixty kids go out for freshmen football, and although I was a skinny 6'1" and 138 pounds, I ended up as the first-string tight end. As awkward, immature freshmen, it would take a couple of years for my teammates and me to evolve into athletes and students—commonly referred to as "Salesian Gentlemen."

One guy on our team, Mike Webb, stood six feet and weighed 210, all muscle. A year older than us, he was a man playing in a boys' league. Mike would go on to achieve All-State status and attend Notre Dame on a football scholarship.

While he was not a standout in football at Notre Dame, in a demonstration of his tough-guy status, he would win the heavyweight boxing title in what was known as the "Bengal Bouts." Just a few years after this, I would receive one of the early shocks of my life when I learned that Mike had dropped dead of a heart attack in a pick-up basketball game. This was one of my first inklings that ominous things could be going on inside an otherwise healthy, athletic body.

As freshman, we won all five of our games at Sallies, and as we developed, it looked like we might join the ranks of Dim Montero's outstanding teams. I looked forward to being coached by Montero, but it was not to be. During that year, he announced he would be leaving Salesianum to become an assistant athletic director and recruiter for the University of Maryland football team. My mentor would be leaving Sallies, so the future of Sallies football and my own place in that world was uncertain.

The new head coach, Wayne Allen, was a Sallies football icon, but only twenty-five years old. Allen had played at Notre Dame, where he had started at guard. I recall that the handsome young man with the dark-rim glasses reminded me of Clark Kent, Superman's alter ego. During all my time with him, I never once heard him use a bad word. Allen showed his displeasure with expressions like "Jiminy Cricket, Reilly!" or "Cheese and crackers, you guys!" I wouldn't see much of that in the NFL.

Over that summer, I joined my Sallies football buddies Tony Nerlinger, Larry Pietropaulo, and Marty Pavlick for trips to the Wilmington YMCA for weightlifting three days a week. If one of us missed a day, there was hell to pay with the other three. Looking back on those days, I know now that we used way too many weights and did too much lifting. But despite violating the weightlifting protocols that I would learn about in college and the pros, I did get a lot stronger and put on some much-needed pounds.

Coach Allen's first year was a tough one, ending with a record of 3–4–3. Mike Webb, now 6'1" and 225 pounds, rose quickly to become the starting fullback. He was soon recognized as one of the most ferocious players in the region.

The Sals played very few in-state opponents at that time, so we had to travel to Washington, Baltimore, and Philadelphia to find them. In many cases, we played against larger schools that also had national reputations. The public schools in our area had formed the Blue Hen Conference, and many of us felt that Sallies was excluded because there was a bias against Catholics. During my time on the team at Sallies, the tide started to turn when a small school in the southwestern part of the county announced they were willing to face the Sals. More about that later.

As a sophomore, I began to work my way into some games as a punter. This was a skill I picked up practicing with a friend from Archmere Academy, a nearby elite Catholic school. I also started to get into some games playing end and caught a few passes, although I never made it across the goal line.

We played our home games across the street from Salesianum at Baynard Stadium. Games under those Friday night lights in front of 5,000 fans were an experience that captivated me. It was everything I dreamed about in my grade school days when I attended games there and I loved everything about it. The allure pushed me to want to wear a Sallies uniform and have those fans (especially the girls) cheering me on.

Having some game time during my sophomore year enabled to me to achieve an early goal—earning a Sallies letter jacket. This garment was particularly important if you wanted to impress the girls at our favorite hangout, The Charcoal Pit. "The Pit," as we called it, was reminiscent of the soda shop from the popular TV show *Happy Days*. Another highlight of our high school social life was being able to attend the Friday night Sallies' dances.

One Friday, when I had a good game and even got banged up a bit, I had the opportunity to show up at the dance with a bandage over my eye to impress the girls.

Regrettably, my father had a rule that we could only attend one dance a month and I had used up my monthly allotment. He would not budge, so instead of being the hero for a night, I headed back to the little house in Blue Rock Manor with Dad. Naturally, when my younger sisters came of age, Dad cracked under pressure and dropped the one-night rule. Unfortunately, it was too late for me.

While the Sals were having a challenging season under the new coach, a small public school in the southwestern corner of New Castle County was on a winning rampage. Outside of Salesianum, the state had never seen anything like the Middletown Cavaliers under coach Bill Billings. They had been undefeated for three seasons and had the audacity to challenge the mighty Sals.

People in Delaware still talk about that game, which we lost 14–13 on a series of razzle-dazzle plays including something most of us hadn't seen since pick-up football—a "Statue of Liberty" play!

I remember leaving the Salesianum parking lot at twilight dressed in everything but our shoulder pads. After nearly an hour drive, we passed through the quaint little town of Middletown, which looked like something out of the deep South. That evening it was like a ghost town with signs in all the windows: "Go Cavaliers, beat Sallies!" When we got to the stadium, we realized that the entire town was at the game.

Losing to Middletown was a big blow to the towering Salesianum football ego, and it happened on my watch. The feeling in my gut that night and in the immediate days ahead was something I never wanted to experience again.

Within weeks following the Middletown loss, we shifted into basketball season and then into baseball. Although Salesianum would become renowned for extraordinary winning streaks and state championships in cross country, soccer, swimming, and even lacrosse, America in the 1960s was still mostly a "three-sport" country, and that's where I focused all my time and energy.

I loved basketball and baseball, and they clearly benefited my overall athletic development. And just as important, it exposed me to other coaches and people who would have a long-term impact on my life, particularly men like our baseball coach, Father Robert Ashenbrenner. But I needed to make sure that I kept up my grades, so I dropped baseball during my last two years in high school and concentrated on football and basketball, knowing that football was my chance for a scholarship.

Good form, bad shorts

‖‖

CHAPTER 5

Am I Ready to Meet My God?

New York, 1979

"You understand … there is a chance you may not survive this surgery."

I n the 1970s, Memorial Sloan Kettering Hospital in New York was renowned as the top cancer hospital in the world. While it certainly stands at the epicenter of the latest advancements in medical science, to be told you must go there for treatment in 1979 meant that this might be your last chance. Founded in 1884 by John Jacob Astor and his wife, Charlotte, Sloan Kettering is synonymous with cutting-edge cancer research and treatment. The name Sloan comes from Alfred Sloan, the man who built General Motors into the largest company in the world. In addition to Sloan, other names affiliated with this institution include Charles Kettering, and John D. and Laurence Rockefeller. Charles Kettering worked for Sloan and was directed by him to bring modern industrial techniques to cancer research. John D. Rockefeller donated the land at 1275 York Avenue, where the hospital stands today.

‖‖

At 5:30 AM on a rainy, chilly, late October morning in 1979, I sat alone at the edge of my bed in the darkness of room 405 at Memorial Sloan Kettering Cancer Center, waiting patiently for a hospital orderly to transport me to pre-op on the second floor.

This was the day that would change my life forever. I was twenty-nine, married, and a father of three small children under the age of four.

Prior to discovering the desmoid tumor that was destroying my left shoulder and strangling the blood supply to my left arm, I was in the best shape of my life and looking to a return to the NFL as a linebacker with three years' experience. As I sat in the darkness trying to grasp the circumstance of this continuous battle, I couldn't help but think this was all just a bad dream, and that I would wake up from another concussion on the field with the stinging smell of a broken ammonia cap beneath my nose.

Unfortunately, this was not a dream. After two operations and nine doctors' opinions, I tried to prepare myself for the worst-case scenario—a forequarter amputation that would result in the loss of my left arm, left shoulder, and at least four ribs. I had already lost my left scapula and clavicle in the earlier surgery. It hadn't worked, and we were now in a race to save my life. It was a two-minute drill with no time-outs.

In the silence and darkness of my room, I started to shiver from the chill and anxiety of this surreal experience. I prayed to God to please help me handle this, and I hoped desperately that maybe they could save my arm.

Suddenly in the middle of praying the Our Father, I looked up and saw a shadowy figure darken my doorway. As soon as I heard his voice, I knew it was Father O'Brien, the Catholic chaplain.

"Kevin, would you like to take communion?"

"Yes, Father, I would."

After communion, I asked Father to stay and pray with me. As he laid both hands on my head, I felt that Christ was with me. I was filled with a calm that reminded me of a quote that I once heard from an Oblate priest: "When God enters a room, fear leaves immediately."

A few minutes later, I was sedated and an orderly appeared with a gurney to take me down to pre-op. There were already four or five people on gurneys in the pre-op area when I arrived, all waiting for an operating room.

Nothing bonds total strangers like facing a life crisis together. Within minutes, each of the six pre-op patients introduced themselves and their reason for surgery on this early October morning.

To my right was Carol from New York City, who was having a biopsy done on a large breast nodule. She appeared to be in her forties, with short brown hair, sparkling blue eyes, and a Mona Lisa smile.

To my left was John, a robust man in his fifties with a deep, raspy voice that betrayed years of smoking. He was a big fellow from Trenton, New Jersey, who looked like he played some football in his day. He was there to have a lung removed. When John heard that I played for the Eagles, he boasted that he was a loyal Giants' fan. I kidded him, "That's nice, your Giants are so bad that they are two years away from being three years away." He laughed.

I leaned over to talk to Carol, who was quietly eavesdropping on our conversation. Carol and I talked briefly about our families and where we were from before the conversation turned to the present reality that we faced. After a long, soul searching pause, she asked me, "Are you scared?"

"Yes, are you?"

"Petrified." Tears welled up in the corner of her eyes. "Would you pray with me?"

Everyone had been quietly listening. John asked the group, "Why don't we all hold hands and say the Lord's Prayer together?"

"I'm Jewish, but I'll be glad to join in if all of you lead," said Adam, who was the last patient in our gurney row.

After we prayed, John continued to hold my left hand. As I looked quizzically at him he said, "I feel privileged to be the last to shake your left hand."

His words hit me. Reality started to really sink in and I couldn't help but stare at my hand. It would be a part of me just a little while longer.

At that point Father O'Brien appeared next to my gurney, just as Carol was whisked away for her surgery while wishing me luck. I was puzzled at Father's reemergence. "Father, you already gave me communion."

"Yes, I know, but I'm here to give you the Anointing of the Sick," he said.

My heart began beating rapidly. Anxiety rose in my throat. As an old Catholic altar boy, I knew that this sacrament used to be called Last Rites. The Last Rites were only administered to the very sick and dying in preparation for death. Father saw the startled look on my face and quickly recovered enough to ask, "Dr. Marcove has been here, hasn't he?"

He had not, but at that very moment Marcove appeared running late as usual. He handed me a document along with a pen, "Sign this," he said. "It was supposed to have been given to you earlier this morning."

It was a two-paragraph letter, but just one sentence is now permanently etched in my mind: "You understand that as an adult patient undergoing this operation, there is a chance you will not survive the surgery."

Signing that document just before they wheeled me toward the operating room made me realize the only thing that really mattered was my relationship with God at that very moment. If I never awoke from surgery, nothing else would matter.

It was as if the fog of life lifted before me. *Am I ready to meet my God?* I asked myself. I said the Catholic prayer, the Act of Contrition, several times with a sense of purpose that I had never known before.

Moments later in the operating room, the anesthesiologist placed a mask over my face, and I drifted off. *"Oh my God, I am heartily sorry for having offended thee, and I detest all my sins...."*

CHAPTER 6

High School Football Success

Wilmington, Delaware, 1968

"I'd be disappointed if we didn't go undefeated!"

s the summer of 1968 faded into late August, twenty-six senior football players were grinding it out with forty underclassmen in grueling double session practices in ninety-degree heat on the Salesianum practice field.

Coming off a 7–1 season, that year's team showed enough promise to go undefeated and join the legendary ranks of the Dim Montero era that produced four undefeated teams. The '68 calendar was loaded with out-of-state teams, leading off with the rough and tough St. James of Chester, Pennsylvania, followed by the best team in the Philadelphia Catholic League, our brother Oblate school, Father Judge.

St. James was a team full of street-smart tough guys from blue-collar families and hardscrabble neighborhoods. Prior to the game, Matt Zabitka, lead sports writer covering Delaware high school sports, interviewed Mike Webb and me. It was the Wednesday before the Friday night battle at Baynard Stadium. During the interview, Zabitka asked me what our expectations were for the upcoming season. Young and inexperienced with the media, I said, "I'd be disappointed if we didn't go undefeated!" Mike then piled on, "We'd like to go unscored upon with our all-senior defense!"

The next morning, there it was in the local paper in black and white...

Sals Seniors Seek Undefeated and Unscored Upon Season

Just after the first period bell, Webb and I were summoned to Coach Allen's office to face a very angry coach.

"Undefeated? Unscored on? Hell, maybe we won't give up a yard to any team this year!" He screamed so loudly at the two of us that I thought the blood vessels in his neck were going to burst. He ordered us not to speak to the media again until after the season.

The coach continued his fiery rant an inch from my face and yelled, "Don't you guys understand that every team on our schedule has Salesianum circled as the team to beat? You guys better wake up!"

St. James came into our house that Friday ready to do battle, and after four quarters of brain rattling defensive hits by both teams, the game ended in a 6–6 tie. While still technically undefeated, we were also humbled and now understood Coach Allen's concerns.

Heading in for the score against St. James

Next up was the 3-0 Father Judge Crusaders, who unlike the Sals, had not yet been scored upon in the early season. Following the scare by St. James, we were laser focused for the match-up with Philadelphia's best, and we won a hard-fought battle 16–0.

Next, we rolled over in-state rival P.S. Dupont, 28–0 for our second straight shutout. Apart from St. John's of Washington, D.C., we basically dominated the rest of our scheduled opponents leading up to the big finale: Salesianum vs. Middletown.

The Middletown Cavaliers had won the first match-up 14–13, we prevailed in the second battle 21–18, and now we were to face off in the rubber match. The Cavaliers were the only barrier standing between us and an undefeated season. The pressure was on!

When we arrived at the Middletown Stadium sixty minutes before kickoff in two buses, half dressed in our uniforms, I thought we were late. The stadium was already packed and there were people camped out on the rooftops of adjacent homes. As in our first meeting, everyone who loved Middletown was at the game, along with the 500 Sallies students who arrived by bus. This definitely had the feel of a Texas Friday night game in the rural farmland of lower Delaware.

After stopping the Cavaliers on their first offensive drive, our quarterback Chuck Dobroski was in single safety to receive the punt. Believing he was at the ten-yard marker on the poorly marked field, he took the ball and retreated two yards to avoid being tackled only to get tripped up at what he thought was the eight-yard line. It wasn't. He was two yards deep into the end zone and it was a safety. Middletown 2, Salesianum 0.

On their next series, Middletown scored the first touchdown and led 9–0. We soon scored, but were behind at halftime 9–7. You could feel the doubt creeping in as we gathered in the locker room. Outside, the Middletown fans kept ringing what seemed to be a thousand cowbells throughout the ten-minute half-time break.

Surprisingly, there was no fire and brimstone pep talk from Coach Allen. Our twenty-seven-year-old head coach calmly settled the team and talked about a new strategy for the second half on offense. He spoke with confidence that we would close the Cavaliers down as the game went on.

Middletown was keying on our All-State fullback Mike Webb and quarterback Dobroski, using one and two-man spies on them and effectively shutting them down. In the second half, Allen switched them up to become decoys and carry after carry went to halfbacks Larry Pietropaulo and Tony Nerlinger. Our defense held, and we won the game going away 32–16.

What a relief! It had been four years, since Salesianum's last undefeated season in 1964. While Mike Webb's forecast of going unscored upon was not realized, our defense had held our opponents to less than a touchdown per game.

When the Delaware All-State Football selections were announced that year, the eleven-man squad was dominated by Salesianum with four first team selections: fullback/linebacker Mike Webb, center/linebacker Charlie Marion, lineman Pat Duffy, and tight end/defensive end, Kevin Reilly. Eleven of my teammates received scholarships to colleges such as Notre Dame, Villanova, Kentucky, and Delaware.

The season and the team that year proved to be a major turning point in my life. It reinforced to me that hard work, discipline, teamwork and a belief in yourself and those around you, could culminate in great success. The true brotherhood that I experienced during my four years at Salesianum, along with the culture of Catholic faith and a "never quit" attitude, would serve me well in the challenges of life ahead. As we say in the locker room, "I got the pride of Salesianum."

Team captain Kevin Reilly (#87) and the
Salesianum 1968 undefeated football team

‖‖

CHAPTER 7

Returning from the Brink

New York, 1979

"You think you got it all?"

It had been four days since the surgery that removed my left arm, shoulder, and four ribs. I only remember bits and pieces of my first day in the Intensive Care Unit. I guess coming out of an eleven-and-a-half-hour operation under heavy anesthesia took up the rest of the day and the pain medication they gave me left me heavily sedated.

Briefly, for only seconds at a time, I would remain conscious, usually followed by an extended period of deep sleep. When I was conscious, I could hear people talking in the background but I couldn't move anything, especially my head.

As my periods of consciousness grew longer and more frequent, I became more aware of my surroundings. My first thought was, *Am I still alive?* Seriously. My head and neck were so strongly locked into position that I couldn't turn my neck to the side. All I could see was white above me. *Was I in heaven or still on earth?* I would wonder. I was on so many drugs that the answer didn't even concern me too much. Then, fighting drowsiness, I would fall back into a coma-like state.

Eventually, I came to long enough to clear my eyes and look at the wall clock to my left. I remember thinking, *I'm still here on earth because there probably aren't any clocks in eternity*, before falling back to sleep once more.

I was suddenly awakened by a strong shooting pain in my lower abdomen. It was on the right side, not the area they had operated on. I wasn't sure why I felt pain on that side. I cried for help. A nurse appeared almost immediately. "Please, can I have some water?"

I was told that I wasn't allowed to have anything by mouth for another twelve hours. They could not risk me vomiting and creating a major problem.

I found out that a drainage tube connected to the area they had amputated was causing the pain in my right abdomen. I was finally conscious of my body, achieving some movement in my legs and being able to lift my head. The most eerie feeling was what I thought was the presence of my left arm and fingers. I could almost believe they had saved my arm since the tingling sensation was so strong.

The nurses explained that I was feeling a "phantom sensation" which I would feel for the rest of my life. They also confirmed that the forequarter amputation had taken place. It had been my second worst-case scenario; the first being not living through the surgery.

Anxiety and increased movement were ratcheting up my pain levels. I was given a morphine shot through the IV in my right arm, then faded back into never-neverland. When I woke up, some of the drains and monitors had been removed. I was even able to walk a little before collapsing back onto my hospital bed. The nurses kept checking my vitals and assessing my condition.

The large bandage on my left shoulder still completely covered the surgery area. It was a little bloodstained and beginning to smell. As I sat in the bed, I began to feel sorry for myself. I had always been proud of what my body could accomplish, but this time it had let me down.

Now that I knew how much had been removed in surgery, I began to think about the future and my family. What kind of father and husband would I be? Would I be able to go back to my sales position at Xerox, or would they put me in the back room, a sad remnant of a man who might make those around him uncomfortable?

I didn't understand my new and severely altered body. I worried if I would be able to run or lift weights. Working out had been a daily part of my life since childhood. Would the rest of me need chemo or radiation after the surgery?

And the most important question of all: Had Dr. Marcove, the brilliant orthopedic surgeon at Sloan Kettering and savior to many a cancer survivor, gotten it all? Had he been able to remove every trace of the desmoid and gain the necessary margins around it to keep it from returning? Since the tumor had already reappeared three times, what guarantee was there that it was finally gone?

I looked up to see the photos of my three small children next to the bed. Brett was two, Erin one, and Brie was an infant. I teared up as I worried that I wouldn't be able to be the father to them I had always wanted to be; teaching them how to play sports or tossing them into the air. I turned the photos face down to shut out my dark thoughts.

At that time, an entourage entered my room led by the man himself, Dr. Marcove. He usually traveled with a nurse and three young interns. As he approached the bed, I went from sad to worried. This man knew better than anyone if I would have a future.

"How are you feeling today, Kevin?"

"A great deal better with some of the tubes and monitors off me."

He seemed pleased with my healing, and then turned his attention to Joan Kaiser, the clinical nurse specialist and lead on my case. She gave a very positive report on my external medical reading, including food intake and walking the floor. They told me my recovery was exceeding the average schedule. Marcove didn't want me to celebrate just yet, however. A cautious doctor who had seen his share of tragedies, he made sure I was aware of what my body had been through.

"I'm happy with the operation. It went well, but as you know, it was over eleven-and-a half hours," he cautioned. "Due to the trauma of losing your left arm, shoulder, and four ribs, you're going to need to take it slowly and get plenty of rest." He explained that the thoracic surgeon who assisted him, Dr. McCormick, replaced the four ribs with plastic ribs and did an incredible job of installing a 6"x7" plate from my neck to my new ribs to protect my vital organs.

In fact, the new synthetic polymer that Dr. McCormick had molded in the operating room was a medical first. The unusual procedure would be written up in a medical journal.

Dr. Marcove then gave me the news I had been waiting for: "I'm pretty sure we got it all," he said.

I couldn't believe it. "You *think* you got it all?" I roared, startling the group. "What happens to me if it comes back again?"

"Settle down, big guy," Marcove responded. "I would have liked to have gotten a few more frozen cultures back from your neck area, but after eleven-and-a-half hours of surgery, you were starting to lose ground. We were worried about your falling vital signs. It was time to wrap up."

He must have seen my face. With unexpected empathy, he lowered his voice and turned towards my bed. "Listen," he offered. "I'm pretty sure we got it all but if by any chance we didn't, I'll keep at it until I do. And you need to believe that."

Keep at it? Where else could he cut? But somehow the message sounded encouraging and I calmed down. Although he wasn't known for his warm and fuzzy bedside manner, the two of us had hit it off and now shared a special bond. I like to think we understood and even grew to like each other. I know I wasn't always at my best in his presence, but there is something powerful about relationships made when you are at the end of your rope.

Hoping to raise my spirits, Marcove informed me, "If you continue to improve at the pace you've been on, I may be able to release you in four days."

The discharge forecast raised my spirits for a little while, but I was still angry and depressed over the shape I was left in. I asked Joan to hold all my phone calls and keep visitors away for the rest of the day. I was still working my head around the future. It was time for me to throw my own pity party.

‖‖

CHAPTER 8

Villanova and the Path to the NFL

Villanova, Pennsylvania 1971–1973

"Kevin, welcome to the Miami Dolphins."

Founded in 1842, Villanova University is a private Catholic school run by the Augustinian order. Located west of Philadelphia on the "Main Line" (named for the former "main line" of the Pennsylvania Railroad), this sprawling suburban area was featured in the 1940 Academy Award-winning movie *The Philadelphia Story* and is home to the historic Merion Golf Club, as well as large mansions and blue bloodlines.

Athletically, Villanova had held national prominence in track and basketball. The lower Division I football program garnered a distant third place. But during the early 1970s, football was on the upswing. Having accepted a scholarship out of Salesianum to play there, I was excited to be a part of the resurgence. The 1970 Wildcat team went 9–2, beating the likes of the University of Maryland, Navy, and Temple.

That 9–2 season was the tenth best in the nation out of 123 Division 1 teams that year. In the following 1971 campaign, the senior dominated team found opponents waiting for the high-flying "Wildcats" and we dropped to a 6–4–1 record. We suffered a narrow 10–7 loss to a streaking Toledo team, a disappointing loss to Division II rival Delaware, and a crushing 42–9 defeat to the University of Houston in the Astrodome.

During that two-year period, two outstanding Villanova athletes emerged as top draft picks in the 1972 NFL Draft. That draft, held on February 1 and 2, 1972, consisted of seventeen rounds of team picks. It concluded with Atlanta head coach and former Philadelphia Eagle Norm Van Brocklin famously yelling to his staff during their last pick in the 17th round, "We want the roughest, toughest SOB in the draft!" They then proceeded to draft actor John Wayne of "Fort Apache State." Van Brocklin's attempt at adding humor to the proceedings failed to impress NFL Commissioner Pete Rozelle. He disallowed the pick.

Another first round selection was future Hall of Famer Franco Harris, who was drafted as the thirteenth pick of the first round by the Pittsburgh Steelers. Eight selections later, the Oakland Raiders drafted Villanova wide receiver Mike Siani as the twenty-first pick.

In the second round and thirty-ninth overall pick, the Dallas Cowboys took Villanova Linebacker John Babinecz. Only Notre Dame and Nebraska had more players drafted in the top forty, with three each.

Villanova football was in "rare air" with a #1 and #2 pick in the 1972 draft. It had never happened before, and it has not happened since. In total, only forty Villanova football players, including the great Howie Long, have been drafted into the NFL since the school's inception. The 1972 draft was an historic year for the team.

Mike Siani was a special athlete. Born and raised in Staten Island, New York, he was a three-letter sports star at New Dorp High School. Measuring 6"3' and 190 pounds, Siani started all three years at wide receiver for the Wildcats football team, while simultaneously starting as shortstop for three years on the university's baseball team. His performance on the baseball diamond made him the #2 pick of the Los Angeles Dodgers that same year.

John Babinecz was born and raised in Pittsburgh. He was a three-year starter as tight end and linebacker for Central Catholic High School, as well as an All-State shot put champion. At 6'2" and 225 pounds, Babinecz was a smart, punishing linebacker with a tackling style that was unmatched in college football at that time.

In 1971, these two outstanding NFL prospects caused a surge in attendance at both Villanova's home and away games. Due to this increase in popularity, yours truly, a 6'2"and 220-pound junior linebacker playing next to Babinecz, began attracting attention as a potential draft pick for 1973.

It is funny how things sometimes work out. Being overshadowed that year by the great Babinecz ultimately played in my favor. On Saturday, November 20, 1971, he was scratched from the lineup thirty minutes before the important Temple game due to a broken hand.

Interception versus Temple, 1972

It was well into the game before NFL scouts began to realize that my number 46 was not number 64, John Babinecz. But they had begun to notice the great game I was having. Although John and I both played inside linebacker in Villanova's 3-4 defense, the defense was designed so that I would slide to nose guard from his inside linebacker position any time Babinecz called a defensive audible just before the snap of the ball. This situation probably occurred forty percent of the time, which left us in a 4-3 defense with Babinecz as the lone middle linebacker.

Due to this defensive change in alignment, Babinecz would average 12-15 tackles a game to my 5-7, since the nose tackle position took on blockers, leaving Babinecz free to chase down the ball carriers. When Babinecz was unable to play that Saturday in November, I was moved to his spot and a senior named Pat Berrang, who didn't play often, replaced me at nose guard.

There were over a dozen NFL scouts in the stands for our final game that season. Babinecz's injury and the number of scouts coming to see him, presented a once-in-a-lifetime opportunity for me to take center stage for the Wildcats defense. Ranging from sideline to sideline I finished the game with seventeen tackles that Saturday. As the afternoon progressed, the scouts realized that the guy playing like number 64, John Babinecz was actually number 46, Kevin Reilly.

That day changed my life. My name was suddenly on the lips of top NFL recruiters, something that might never had occurred if Babinecz had played that day. I was now on the radar for the NFL prospect list.

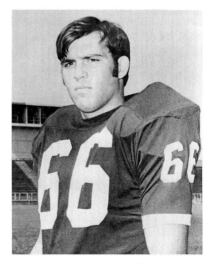

Villanova Wildcat

The following year, 1972, I was named co-captain of a Villanova team that had lost fourteen senior starters and was facing its toughest schedule in decades. The season's lineup included West Virginia University, the University of Kentucky, Boston College, Temple University, and the University of Maryland. Our year was a bust as we struggled offensively, scoring only 100 points in ten games and ending with a dismal 2–9 record.

Despite our losing record, I was fortunate enough to be named to the first team All-East squad at linebacker and received an invitation to play in the annual North-South Shrine College All-Star Game in Miami on Christmas Day. I was also still in the running as an NFL prospect.

In 1972, the nationally broadcast Shrine game was more than another college football game. Since this was before the advent of the formal NFL Combine program in which prospects are evaluated in a multi-day camp environment, all twenty-six NFL teams at the time were on site to put us through basic drills and check all our personal data such as height, weight, speed, and so on. I was excited about the opportunity to play in the game, but was more focused on making an impression on the scouts.

Soon after we arrived at the Ivanhoe Hotel in Miami, we were summoned to a meeting with the coaching staff. Coaching the North team was the legendary Duffy Daugherty of Michigan State, assisted by another legend in his own right, Bob DeMoss of Purdue. In addition to being a great coach, Dougherty was known for some of his famous sayings like, "A tie is like kissing your sister" and "When you are playing for the national championship, it is not a matter of life and death—it's more important than that."

We settled down quickly as Daugherty grabbed some chalk and went up to the board in the front of the room. Most of us carried pen and paper and were poised to write down his every word. The first thing I noticed, to my surprise, was that Daugherty had a speech impediment. He stuttered through his comments. As he began to write on the chalkboard, he said the first thing he wanted to do was to review the rules for camp. They were:

RULE #1 – IF YOU ENTER A BAR OR TAVERN IN THIS TOWN AND YOU SEE ME OR COACH DEMOSS YOU ARE TO LEAVE IMMEDIATELY!

RULE #2 – OBEY ALL RULES ABOVE!

After the laughter died down, he told us we were down there to have fun and perform for the NFL scouts and not to get hurt. After a slight pause he said, "Oh, and I do expect to win the game,"

As I think back on it today, it must have been karma that I would be in Miami for the game. In addition to the practice sessions, our itinerary included a trip to a Miami Dolphins division play-off game at the Orange Bowl. Driving home the point about the status of our Shrine game coaches was the fact that both the Dolphins' quarterback Bob Griese and Cleveland Browns' quarterback Mike Phipps had been coached by Bob DeMoss. Miami would prevail in a close game 20–14 and go on to the only undefeated season in NFL history.

On another day in Miami, my Uncle Jack, who had come to town to follow me, took me out to a Dolphins' practice. Since it was playoff time, the practice was closed to the public so we stood out of range behind a cyclone fence. As we stood there watching, a figure broke away from the players and came over to us. It was Coach Don Shula. He politely informed us that the practice was closed and we would have to leave. My uncle jumped in to tell him I was an NFL prospect in town for the Shrine game. Shula was unmoved and politely repeated that he had to ask us to leave.

In addition to doing well during my workout with the scouts, I was fortunate to have a great Shrine game. I made eight unassisted tackles and recovered two fumbles, one of which I could have easily scored on but, under special rules for the game, I could not advance the ball. So, with the big game behind me, I was full of lofty expectations for the upcoming NFL draft.

When draft day rolled around at the end of January, the local sports writers had me slotted to be picked somewhere between the sixth and twelfth round in a draft with seventeen rounds overall. There was one other Wilmington native son expected to be drafted, Jim Kraft, who made first team All-American as a center for coach Bear Bryant's Crimson Tide. One of the best athletes in the history of Delaware, Kraft was also the state's top high school wrestler.

The previous year, 1972, I had joined in the campus draft-day activities in anticipation of the selection of both Mike Siani and John Babinecz. The celebration started early and then went late into the night after they were picked in the first and second rounds. In my case, in 1973, teammates and friends gathered in my dorm and broke out the beer as the first round started around noon. The party was going full tilt by 4:00 PM, but I was not going to touch a beer until it all became official. But there was no mention of Reilly in the fourth or fifth rounds.

By time they made it half way through the sixth round, everyone began to drift away to watch the Wildcat basketball game set to tip off at Jake Nevin Fieldhouse. My name failed to come up in the sixth round, so I followed the others to the game. I was disappointed that I did not go in the sixth and now worried I might not be drafted at all. Maybe the scouts just didn't like my skinny legs holding up my 220-pound body.

I joined some other friends in the section under the basket where I could see the doors to the athletic department offices on the upper deck. Sitting rather dejected before half-time in the game, I suddenly noticed Villanova defensive coordinator John Rosenberg and athletic director Art Mahan trying to get my attention. John was holding up seven fingers and mouthing the words which I could barely make out, "Miami Dolphins."

I dashed up to the office, and they handed me a phone. On the other end was the Dolphins' director of player personnel, Bobby Bethard. I recalled that Bethard was there at the North–South Shrine game. He quickly gave me the good news and said, "There is someone else with me that wants to speak to you."

"Kevin," said the legendary coach of the Dolphins, Don Shula. "Welcome to the Miami Dolphins. I want you to know that I am very familiar with you and your background. I have walked the corridors of Salesianum School in Wilmington, and I look forward to seeing you soon." Shula would later share with me that while he was coaching at the University of Virginia he came to Wilmington in an attempt

Nova teammates Mike Sunday, Drew Gordon, Duane Holland, Tony Prazenica and Kevin Reilly

to recruit two Salesianum standouts, Jack Mulvena and Tommy Hall. He returned to the school in 1964 as head coach of the Baltimore Colts to speak at the Salesianum sports banquet.

I was the 160th player to be taken in the draft. When I hung up from Shula, I immediately called my parents to give them the good news. While I was on the phone, the word began to spread through the fieldhouse. Making my way back to my seat, everyone began shaking my hand or high fiving me just as the announcement came across the public address system, "Kevin Reilly has just been drafted in the seventh round by the world champion Miami Dolphins!" The Wildcat basketball team, led by my friend (and future Atlanta Hawk) Tom Inglesby, stopped their second-half warm-up drill and all came over to shake my hand.

In just a few minutes, I had gone from down in the dumps to the toast of the town. What an incredible feeling! After the game, we all headed out to Kelly's Bar in Bryn Mawr. Just like Mike Siani and John Babinecz the year before, I enjoyed my draft party well into the next morning.

CHAPTER 9

The Visitor and the Running Back

New York, 1979

"Kevin, you must promise me that you won't quit on anything until you try it three times!"

ollowing the visit from Dr. Marcove, questions continued to mount about the ordeal that lay ahead. When my nurse Joan Kaiser entered the room, she knew things were getting to me. She was not only an excellent nurse, but she had become a good friend during my first Sloan Kettering operation the year before.

We talked for a while. After calming me down, I asked her to keep visitors and phone calls away for the rest of the day so I could clear my head about my new situation.

About an hour into my isolated strategy session, an older gentleman with a white hospital jacket and credentials stood at my doorway. He wasn't a doctor or intern, and I didn't recognize him as anyone I had met previously at the hospital. He was in his mid-sixties with a full head of white hair. He had a congenial smile as he knocked and entered the room.

Approaching my bed, I could clearly see that although I had no idea who he was, we had something in common—he was an amputee. His name was Frank, and he was a WWII veteran, missing his left arm from the shoulder down. He had lost his arm in combat and was a hospital volunteer who helped counsel arm amputees like me.

Frank was pleasant, and he clearly wanted to be helpful and put me at ease. He brought me a special knife designed for amputees that would allow me to cut most any meat served with one hand. He also brought a pillow-like device that was a soft, temporary prosthetic shoulder.

I asked him why I needed a temporary one when I was scheduled to be fitted for a permanent one in ninety days?

"Kevin, my boy," he said. "You don't want to have your jacket sleeve down around your ankles when you leave the hospital. You want to leave here a little buttoned up and preserve a little sense of dignity."

I thought, *Just a few years ago, I was tackling the likes of O.J. Simpson, John Riggins, Larry Csonka, and Joe Namath, and now I need to worry about my dignity when leaving a Manhattan hospital?*

Frank then asked me about my job and what I wore to work each day. I told him I wore a business suit with a shirt, tie, and dress shoes. He showed me a pair of dress shoes he was wearing with the laces secured with a velcro flap. "You're going to have to get these shoes with the velcro flap with pre-tied laces because you'll never be able to tie your shoes again," he informed me. "It can't be done. Believe me, I've been trying for thirty-five years."

Continuing with his list of things that could not be done with one hand, Frank showed me his clip-on tie and recommended picking up a supply of them because I would never be able to tie my own necktie. Finally, he asked me about exercise, mentioning that amputees were inclined to significant weight gain during recovery. When I said that I liked to run for enjoyment and weight control, he advised against it, telling me that I would experience issues due to unequal weight distribution, which would lead to disc problems.

Although Frank was there for support, he had unfortunately added to my growing depression and sinking self-esteem. After he left, I began to worry about the long list of things that I hadn't even considered were going to become serious limitations in my new, one-arm life.

While pondering those other challenges, I was interrupted by Joan. I had a telephone call that I should take. "Please," I begged. "I really don't want to talk to anybody right now." She insisted. When she told me who it was, I changed my mind.

It was former Pittsburgh Steeler Rocky Bleier. A college football star at Notre Dame, Bleier had achieved success in the NFL after recovering from severe injuries he received in combat in Vietnam with the 196th Light Infantry Brigade in 1969. Bleier's book, *Fighting Back*, detailed his struggles after being told by doctors that even if he recovered enough to walk, he would never run or play football again.

We had a great talk and at the end, Rocky told me, "Kevin, have any of the doctors, nurses, or rehab people been in to tell you about your limitations?"

I told him about the well-meaning volunteer who came to see me that day and had actually depressed the hell out of me. Rocky listened intently as I explained Frank's visit. With a voice and demeanor of a Marine drill instructor he ordered me, "You must promise me that you won't quit on anything until you try it three times."

"Rocky, I appreciate your enthusiasm and positive attitude," I said. "But I think old Frank is a little more of an expert on being an amputee than you or me."

"Experts built the Titanic and amateurs built the ark," Rocky shot back at me. "Experts can be wrong!"

Rocky wouldn't let me go until I promised him that I would not let anyone set boundaries for me and that I would continue to focus on the big goals that I had before my amputation. I promised.

"You are going to face hundreds of situations where you can't do something at first," Rocky said. "Instead of just counting to ten before retaking the challenge in front of you, I want you to recite a little poem that I'm going to send you. If you repeat this after each failure, I think you will find it more meaningful than counting to ten."

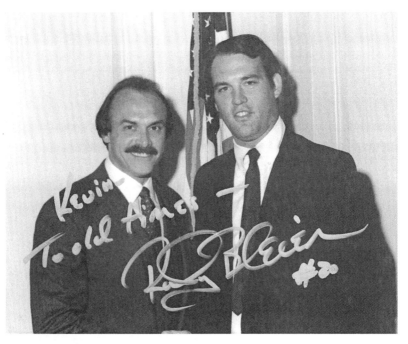

With Rocky Bleier at 1983 Wilmington Vietnam Memorial dedication

Here is what he sent me:

"A Winner's Creed"

If you think you are beaten,
You are;
If you think you dare not,
You don't;
If you'd like to win,
But think you can't,
it's almost a cinch
You won't.

If you think you'll lose
You're lost.
For out in the world
We find
Success begins
With a person's faith;
It's all in the state of mind.

Life's battles don't
Always go
To the stronger or
Faster hand;
They go to the one
Who trusts in God
and always thinks
"I CAN."

Rocky said he was going to follow up on my progress and reiterated, "Do not let other people set the bar of what you can and can't do. That is your job and only your job."

I knew he was right. *Thank you God, for sending Rocky Bleier into my life at that crucial hour.* He changed my whole perspective and mindset.

I have had other opportunities to spend time with Rocky, including one particularly inspiring event only a few years after the surgery. I had asked Rocky to speak at the Vietnam Memorial dedication in Wilmington on November 11, 1983. Members of the committee had considered a number of noteworthy keynote speakers, including President Reagan. But when someone suggested Rocky Bleier, the veterans on the committee made him their top pick. He was the guy who served in the rice paddies and mountain jungles with them when so many others had avoided the draft and the controversial war.

CHAPTER 10

||||||||||||||||||||||||||||||||||||||||||||||||||||||||||||||||||||||||||||||||||||||||||||||||||||||

Welcome to the NFL!

Miami, Florida, 1973

"Young man, we have our own equipment!"

It was ten days before the Dolphins regular season opener against the San Francisco 49ers, and the latest depth chart was posted to the team's bulletin board.

My pulse quickened as my eyes scrolled down the page. There it was. My name was listed on all six special teams: kickoff, kickoff return, punt, punt return, field goal, and extra point.

Some of the veterans were starting to congratulate me on making the team—the most elite in the NFL. It appeared that Coach Shula had decided to keep three rookies: quarterback Don Strock (drafted in the fifth round out of Virginia Tech), Bo Rather (drafted in the seventh round out of Michigan), and me. I exhaled and began to think of myself as a member of the Super Bowl champion Dolphins. But this was the NFL, so I knew anything could happen with ten days to go before the season began.

I was right. No sooner did I breathe a sigh of relief when things began to unravel. Defensive coordinator Bill Arnsbarger got my attention by saying, "Reilly, right after breakfast, Coach Shula wants to see you in his office." He then added the kiss of death, "And bring your playbook."

Like the oft-repeated line out of a Mafia movie, "It's not personal, it's just business!" I immediately lost my appetite. Completely deflated, I walked back to the dorm to retrieve my playbook. I did not fail to notice the stares of the other players as I crossed the parking lot to Shula's office. Fellow linebackers Larry Ball and Doug Swift quickly jogged over to me to say good-bye and good luck, only reinforcing my feeling of dread.

Nine grueling weeks had been spent on twice-a-day practices in the sweltering Florida heat and humidity along with hours spent learning the hybrid "53 Defense." There was also the pounding I took from All-Pro offensive linemen Larry Little, Jim Langer, Bob Kuchenberg—and coming out of the backfield Jim Kiick and the human battering ram named Larry Csonka. I had come so close.

I wondered what had happened in the last couple days to have them sour on me. I learned later that it was NFL politics. Defensive end Bruce Bannon, the New York Jets number five pick out of

Talking strategy with Jim Kiick in a Dolphins pre-season game

Penn State, was trying to convert to linebacker and had just been released. Deemed too small for defensive end, he also struggled as a corner linebacker. Unfortunately for me, Joe Paterno had made a personal call to Don Shula and convinced him that Bannon would be a perfect fit for the "53" backup position behind Bob Matheson. It's tough when one legendary coach calls another and makes the case for the other guy. There was no chance for a rebuttal.

A big positive that came out of the nine-week long "hell week" with the world champion Dolphins was that I received some great individual coaching on technique, and I also learned the NFL's most complex defense.

Leaving Shula's office, Coach Arnsbarger approached and took me aside. A cold, hard perfectionist, Arnsbarger may have been the last man I would have expected to show some humanity at that moment. I was completely surprised when he put his hands on my shoulders, looked me directly in the eye and said, "Look here, look at me. You can play in this league. Believe that. Be patient, and somebody will pick you up."

That was the first nice thing I heard Arnsbarger say since I had come into camp, and it helped to take the sting out of getting fired for the first time in my life.

Later at the airport, I called my agent Jerry Kapstein to inform him that I was now unemployed. He too assured me that I was sure to be picked up by a team in the next couple weeks. He promised to make some calls.

However, I was soon to realize that getting cut before the opening of the season was the worst time to try to catch on with another team. By then, all the coaches and teams were totally focused on game plans and strategies as they planned for opening day. They would check the waiver wire (where all cut players' names are carried) only if they needed a player due to injury. A player picked up a week before the first game can't really be effective until they learn a particular team's offensive or defensive systems.

Even if a team must field an inferior player, "the devil they know is better than the devil they don't know."

I caught a flight out of Miami to my parents' home in Delaware to begin the waiting game. A week went by, then two, and still no word from Jerry Kapstein, who seemed to be ducking my calls. At that point, I realized that I was probably on the bottom rung on the ladder of pro athletes that he represented.

As I learned this lesson the hard way, every morning into week three and four of the NFL season, I semi-tolerated a steady stream of advice from my father. "Why don't you go up to the Eagles practice and talk to head coach Mike McCormack and see if he needs a linebacker?" he advised over and over. "That's what I would be doing instead of sitting on my ass waiting for that damn agent to call!"

My father's badgering got so bad that to prove to him what an idiotic and unprofessional idea that was, I decided to do exactly that, just to prove he was wrong. This was not some movie from the 1930s where the kid comes off the sandlot to make the team. This was the NFL, the biggest professional sport in the country. I couldn't wait to report to him about what a humiliating experience this would prove to be. So off to Veterans Stadium I went that Wednesday morning, wondering if I could even get past security.

Acting as NFL as I could and sporting Miami Dolphins' logos on everything, I managed to convince two security guards I was there for a try out. I then sat inconspicuously in the stands watching two hours of practice.

As the team was leaving the field and the ball boys were picking up the equipment, I hustled down the stadium steps, hopped the fence and made a beeline for Coach McCormack. He was discussing practice with receivers' coach Boyd Dowler, the former All-Pro receiver for Vince Lombardi's great Packer teams.

At the first opening I saw, I jumped in. Not sure where this sudden out-of-character motivation came from, and hoping I didn't make a complete fool out of myself, I sputtered out the words, "Coach, my name is Kevin Reilly. I played linebacker at Villanova and was just recently released by the Dolphins. Is there any way that I could get a tryout? I could even bring my own helmet." I must have sounded like Ralphie in the movie *A Christmas Story*, pleading with Santa Claus for a BB gun.

McCormack, a former four-time All-Pro tackle with the Cleveland Browns, was in his first year as head coach of the Eagles. I could feel my face flush red as McCormack laughed and said, "Young man, we have our own equipment." But he seemed to take my interruption in stride and quickly summoned over the Eagles top scout, former All-Pro defensive tackle from the New York Giants, Jim Katcavage.

Sweating bullets and feeling a little foolish standing there, the two coaches talked out of earshot. After what seemed like an eternity, the two men approached me. McCormack introduced "Kat" and said, "Kevin, be up here tomorrow at 8:00 AM and Kat and Walt Michaels, our linebacker coach will put you through a workout to see if we can use you."

Did I just hear this man right? The next few words exchanged remain a blur but I expect I said, "See you tomorrow." Stunned, I turned around and walked out of the stadium, quickening my pace to get into my car and out of there before somebody changed their mind.

As soon as I got on the road, I kicked myself for not asking what sort of workout they had planned. Should I bring turf cleats or sneakers? Would weightlifting be involved? Was there a slot open on the "taxi squad"?

Then it struck me, *What will I say to my father?* I had only gone through this exercise to prove him wrong. I soon walked into his liquor store and told him what had happened. There was no lecture, no "I told you so" or anything like that. He just said, "If you make the team, just make sure that damn agent of yours doesn't get a dime!"

The next morning, I arrived at the Eagles locker room at 7:30 and received official Eagles whites: a t-shirt, jock strap, shorts, socks, and an empty locker. I suited up, and at 8:00 sharp Kat and Walt took me out on the field and ran me through three forty-yard sprints, backpedaling drills, ball catching drills, and one set of bench presses of 225 pounds. The entire process took forty minutes.

After we finished, they told me to go shower and that they would meet me in the locker room in twenty minutes. I was showered, dressed, and sitting in the locker stall in fifteen, holding my breath! As I waited and looked around, I noticed I was being eyeballed by the early-bird players who clearly wondered who I was. Suddenly, McCormack and Michaels came out of the coaches' room and approached me.

"Kevin, we'd like to sign you to the practice squad, where you will be paid weekly," McCormack said. "You up for that?"

"Sure!" I answered.

He instructed me to show up the next morning at 8:00. "We'll sign you up, and Walt will give you a playbook. Pick up your equipment and plan to attend our morning meetings and practice with the team. Capish?"

"Capish!" I replied.

Two weeks later, wide receiver Ben Hawkins broke his leg. The team needed special team players, so they signed me to a two-year contract. Elevated to the team, I would play in my first NFL game on October 28, 1973 against the Dallas Cowboys at home.

Who needed an agent when I had a caring, no-nonsense father giving me guidance; someone who knew the shortest distance between two points was a straight line and straight talk. Now, I was officially a Philadelphia Eagle, fulfilling a lifelong dream. It was something that would never have happened without that guy in the liquor store.

CHAPTER 11

A Linebacker's Touch

New York, 1979

"Well, Tick, at least you've got two good knees!"

The morning of the sixth day after the operation was different from the full day that I had spent in intensive care and the days recovering in my hospital room. The last drainage tube was gone. It had been tucked into the massive incision that required more than a hundred stitches to close. My IVs were also gone, along with the dreaded catheter.

I have discovered over the years that several Reilly family members are afflicted with a mild case of claustrophobia. Following the surgery, I felt like I was in a kind of bondage. With all the tubes and needles latched onto me, I was unable to move freely without getting something tangled on my remaining arm or medical device.

The tubes served as a kind of timeline, each one being removed as I gradually progressed from standing by the bed on day two, to taking five steps to the door and back on day three. Each day felt like a miracle.

On the fourth day, I took a walk around the floor with the last IV attached. That was nothing compared to the fifth day, when I circled the floor for the first time free of all the devices weighing me down. That was also the last day I received morphine shots, which had helped considerably as I stumbled around the hospital floor circuit.

Twice a day since coming out of surgery, I had received morphine shots. At times, the pain was unbearable. It wasn't just the cutting and exposing of raw nerves. Some of the worst pain came from the tubes piercing my body. The morphine shots would take me from a pain level of nine or ten to nirvana in three to five minutes.

Today, my pain reliever would be Tylenol with codeine pills. I was told that three to five days is the limit for a recovering patient to receive morphine due to its addictive nature. I can believe that!

I knew the nurses got a kick out of me moaning and complaining about the pain one minute and smiling and chatting the next. Once, I even stepped off my bed and "mooned" everyone in the room.

Day six was to be my breakthrough day. Dr. Marcove had been so impressed with my recovery the day before that he had told me if I continued to progress at that rate, I would be released by the eighth day. That was all I needed to hear to focus all my efforts.

Day eight was cemented in my mind as the departure date. All I had to do was keep improving by eating, exercising, and getting my existing fever to under 100. *I can do this!* I told myself. Once I am focused on a target, my competitive streak comes out. I drew on the linebacker's creed for sucking it up, gutting it out, and getting it done.

The day began with my new pain pills and a breakfast of cold scrambled eggs, toast, and fruit. I had no appetite and my taste buds had all gone south, but I got breakfast down and began laps around the hospital corridor. The goal was for eight to ten that morning, and I was optimistic about my chances.

At last, an escape plan from the hospital was firmly in place. Soon, I would be home with my wife and family. My strength and motivation grew every day. I also expected to be able to shower for the first time since the surgery, in honor of some friends who were planning to visit that afternoon. My remaining bandages were also to be removed.

My visitor was one of my best friends, former Eagle teammate John Bunting. John was the starting outside linebacker for the Eagles. He and his wife, Renee, were coming to take me out to dinner. I was excited to see them, although I wondered how they would react to what they would see. I was not a pretty sight.

As the afternoon grew late, I still wore blood-stained bandages. "Why can't I take these off now?" I complained to the nurses. They nodded sympathetically but would not back down. They said I had to wait until John arrived. Instead of the promised shower, they gave me a sponge bath.

Me with John Bunting at his induction to the Wilmington NC Hall of Fame

At 6:00 PM, I sat on the edge of my bed wearing a pair of dress slacks, shoes, and socks. My temporary prosthetic shoulder lay on the bed. It was soft like a pillow, and it would attach with a velcro strap to my missing left shoulder. I was clean-shaven for the first time in days. While I had deodorant on, I still smelled from the rank mound of bandages that resembled the original shape of my left shoulder.

I was as anxious to get out of the hospital as a NASCAR driver from a fiery crash. Finally, after what seemed an eternity, John and Renee appeared in the doorway, dressed casually for a night (or at least an hour) on the town.

"Let's get this show on the road," I told my nurse, Joan Kaiser. All I wanted to do was to get down to the street to mix with "real people" with everyday problems, hear the noise of the city, and get a beer.

Joan whispered quick instructions to John. He nodded and waved me over. We moved to the bathroom just like we broke from an Eagles defensive huddle; quickly and with a sense of purpose.

Inside the bathroom, I faced John as he began to remove the tape and gauze from the front of my chest. He gingerly pulled away the tape from white skin caked with week-old blood. John sucked in his breath, then paused and gave me a nod of encouragement. As he pulled the tape from my chest, his lips pursed and his nose wrinkled. I realized he was holding his breath.

In a few moments, the front side was done and I turned as John painstakingly peeled the gauze and tape from the back of my left shoulder. For a strong guy in a violent sport, he was surprisingly gentle. After another full minute, the entire oversized bandage was ready to go.

He took the mass of tape and gauze off my left side. I looked in the mirror and didn't really comprehend what I was looking at. My arm and shoulder were gone and skin had been sewn back across the upper quarter of my chest creating a direct slope from my neck nearly to my waist.

I was not as shocked about what I saw as what I didn't see. It was as if someone was playing a bad joke on me—taking a picture and cutting out most of what used to be the left side of my upper body. I was the incredible vanishing man.

I stared incredulously at the emptiness as John's eyes bulged out, riveted on the space that should have been there. He was looking at the nothingness of my left arm, shoulder, and four missing ribs. Seconds went by and neither one of us spoke.

John looked down at the bandage, then back at me, "Well, Tick, at least you've got two good knees!" This would become a legendary quote within our family. The "Tick" moniker was a nickname I had been labeled with by some of my Eagle pals during my playing days.

And you know what? It was something. It was positive and it was true. After sixteen years of football, from fifth grade to three years in the NFL, I had never had knee surgery—a rarity for a professional linebacker. Yet, the statement was so "out there" that we both started laughing.

To be honest, if we hadn't laughed, we would have cried. Now I knew why Joan Kaiser had wanted John Bunting to be there with me. Joan knew I was going to need a good friend to be there when I viewed the new version of me for the first time.

"Well, Tick, you always wanted to be ambidextrous, now you are," John joked as Renee buttoned up my shirt. I was completely dressed for the first time in over a week and headed for the real world.

Soon, we were walking the streets of New York. It might have been only a couple of blocks, but I felt alive for the first time in a long time. There was no tube, no hospital, and no bandages. I didn't feel much pain, which I may have been suppressing or was just the effect of the meds.

We passed normal people rather than sick patients in the hospital corridors. They were dressed in normal clothing, moving quickly with a sense of purpose and totally unaware of my missing limb. Were they blind, preoccupied, unfocused, or just being kind? I didn't know what to think as one after the other passed me without eye contact or even a nod.

As we entered the restaurant. I did get a few stares when we were escorted to our table. I thought, "Kev, old boy, you better get used to stares, just wait until you go the Jersey Shore. Hell, little kids will probably faint!"

John, Renee, and I ordered beers, which I couldn't wait to drink. Unfortunately, it was a bit of a disappointment, tasting weak with a metal aftertaste. I ate very little but thoroughly enjoyed the company and atmosphere.

I faded quickly and soon actually wanted to get back to my hospital bed. We were at dinner for perhaps an hour-and-a-half, but it took a toll on me. I fell into a deep sleep that night with a smile on my face. It had been a great day.

CHAPTER 12

Flying with the Eagles

Philadelphia, 1974

"And now ... Captain of the Special Teams ...
from Villanova University ... Kevin Reilly!"

N FL labor unrest dominated the 1974 pre-season. The players went on strike July 1, and I found myself walking a picket line instead of tackling running backs. Since several linebackers did not join the strike, I was seriously jeopardizing my marginal status on the team. Fortunately, the strike ended in mid-August, and I headed back to practice just as we were preparing to take on the 1974 Super Bowl champion Pittsburgh Steelers in a pre-season contest at Veterans' Stadium. On my first day back, I was placed at middle linebacker, a position I had played in college but not yet in the NFL. It was a tough week of practice as I worked to learn the position quickly and get back into football condition.

On game day, I expected to play on all the special teams for a half and at middle linebacker for a quarter. Through the first half, Terry Bradshaw and the Steelers starting team were having their way with the Eagles defense, and we found ourselves down 28–7. But we were ready when the Pittsburgh back-up squads took the field for the second half. During the intermission, linebacker coach Walt Michaels approached me and said, "Reilly, you are going to replace Bergey for the rest of the game. He has a tight hamstring, and we don't want to risk an injury." I was a bit stunned. I certainly wasn't expecting to play an entire half at middle linebacker against the world champions, especially after only a week of preparation at the position. Welcome to the NFL—again!

The Steelers second team offense was not the same Bradshaw-led juggernaut we faced in the first half, and our defense was able to hold them on the first three series—three downs and out. Our offense also began to crank up and put points on the board. As we headed into the fourth quarter, we were down 28–21 and our defense continued to hold, allowing only two first downs. Running on instinct and pure adrenalin, I was having a pretty good game against the Steelers' second and third teams. With little time on the clock, our offense scored again and the game appeared to have ended in a tie at 28. To the surprise of nearly everyone, though, the officials were calling us back onto the field. It turned out that during the off-season the NFL decided to institute a new "sudden death" overtime period to break ties.

As we were buckling up again, the Steelers won the toss and elected to receive. Against our somewhat off-balance special team squad, they returned the kick-off all the way to the Eagles five-yard line. I quickly huddled up the team for our goal-line defense as Pittsburgh brought out the big guns to finish us off. I found myself looking across the line at Terry Bradshaw, Franco Harris, Rocky Bleier, and the rest of the Steeler Super Bowl championship offense.

As the middle linebacker, my job in the goal-line defense was to cover halfback Franco Harris coming out of the backfield. Out of Penn State, Franco Harris was one of the most recognized players in the league following an extraordinary catch in a playoff game in 1972 against the Oakland Raiders, a play that became known as the "Immaculate Reception." The first play was a sweep to Harris angling towards the right sideline. I noticed big #32's first step and broke through a hole in the offensive line. The 6'2", 235 pound star was on his horse, but so was I, and I caught him at the four-yard line. He fought to hold me off with a stiff arm, but I pulled him down at the four for only a one-yard gain.

On the next play, Bradshaw tried the left side, handing off to Harris again. I beat my blocker and hit the big back in stride as he tried to turn upfield and threw him for a one-yard loss. It was now third and goal from the five. Center Mike Webster snapped the ball to Bradshaw, and as he dropped back I could see Franco hold his arms to receive what was clearly going to be a draw play. I slid by Webster and as Harris started to turn up the middle, I hit him waist high for another loss. While we had held them with my moment of pre-season glory, the Steelers kicked an easy field goal and thus prevailed in the game 31–28.

The next morning, a Philadelphia sports columnist wrote: *During the overtime goal-line stand, the Eagles linebacker stopped Franco Harris on three consecutive runs. Last year, we didn't have a middle linebacker that could do that and now it appears we have two—Bill Bergey and Kevin Reilly.* More importantly, coach Mike McCormack singled me out in the locker room after the game for my linebacker play and the

goal-line stand. Almost desperate to make the team heading into that pre-season game, I had sealed the deal courtesy of one of the league's most prominent players.

As the 1974 season began to take shape I was seeing limited time

With Franco Harris and Arnold Palmer, 1985

at the linebacker spot, but I was able to establish myself as a key member and captain of the Eagles special teams. I was hanging in with the big leaguers when on September 23 the Eagles were scheduled to play the Dallas Cowboys on ABC's *Monday Night Football*. The Cowboys were on an eleven-game winning streak against the Birds. They hadn't lost a game to the Eagles since October 29, 1966 at Franklin Field.

There was no question that the dominant Cowboys looked down on their division opponents as a sub-par team. This arrogance naturally enraged the Eagles fan base, who were fiercely proud of their team. The tension between the teams in recent years had steadily increased to the point where fights were breaking out at tailgates every time the teams met.

If you were raised as an Eagles fan, one of the first things you were taught was to hate Dallas. However, "America's Team" had the wins to support their bragging rights and an air of superiority. That was finally about to change that Monday night on national television.

In addition to new head coach, Mike McCormack, the 1974 team featured a couple of hired guns to lead the offense and defense. One of those new acquisitions was Bergey, who had starred at middle linebacker for the Cincinnati Bengals. The other was All-Pro quarterback Roman Gabriel. These two superior players were leaders, and they knew how to win.

For the first time in years, there was hope that the Eagles had more than a chance at a win, and every Eagles fan made a silent wish that this would be the year they defeated the Cowboys. And on *Monday Night Football*, the whole country would be watching. As leader of the special teams, I knew this would be the night our unit would be called upon to rise above.

An hour before game time, I sat in my locker along "linebacker row" quietly padding my forearms like a boxer before a fight, when I heard my name called by special teams' coach Dick LeBeau. LeBeau, then just thirty-seven but a fourteen-year veteran of the Detroit Lions and an All-Pro defensive back, was in his second season as an NFL coach.

This wily veteran of the NFL knew when the conditions were right for a heavyweight boxing match, and he sensed one in the air that night. He walked quickly in my direction and calmly asked me to round up the kickoff team and gather them in the meeting room, right off the locker room. "I'll see you in five minutes," he ordered.

Clearly something was up. This had never happened before. What could be the problem? As the eleven men gathered, everyone was curious. The door opened and LeBeau entered. He stood in front of the squad as he quietly closed the door behind him so as not to disturb the others in the locker room gearing up for the game.

"Gentlemen," he said. "This is your lucky day. I've just been informed that the special teams are going to be introduced on national television instead of the offense or defense."

I'm still not sure who made the call that night, but it seemed to have an enormous impact on the Philly fan base. The upper levels of Veterans Stadium were full of blue collar fans—union workers, plumbers, carpenters, steelworkers, and dock workers, who had helped develop Vet Stadium's reputation for rowdy behavior. They naturally seemed to identify with the wedge busting no name "suicide squads" who hurtled themselves down the field looking for the big hit to bring up the crowd. Whoever had made that call, knew that the "twelfth man" (the crowd) could be the deciding factor in a game like this.

Everyone was completely psyched. The Eagles kickoff team was lined up, one behind the other in the tunnel leading out to the field. I was last in the lineup. As I buckled my helmet following the national anthem, I felt the adrenaline pumping through my veins and my heart pounding against my shoulder pads. The Eagle faithful, tailgating since noon, cheered wildly. Bobby Picard, my fellow wedge-buster, turned to me and banged his facemask against mine and let out a primal scream. "Game on!"

It didn't take long for the fans to get it. By the time the third player was announced, the noise was deafening. We could barely hear the announcer over the roars greeting our special team. With each team member announced, the noise grew louder. And then it was time for #52, Philly's homegrown football player who'd been raised an Eagles fan since birth. "And now … captain of the special teams … from Villanova University … Kevin Reilly!"

I sprinted from the edge of the tunnel to the fifty-yard line where my teammates were setting personal vertical leap records. I couldn't remember my feet touching the ground. I was in a haze of noise and emotion as fans screamed at the top of their lungs, and the lights shone down on the field.

We won the coin toss and elected to kickoff. From the start of the game, the Cowboys didn't know what hit them! Our defense, led by four of the toughest linebackers in the NFL, Bill Bergey, Frank LeMaster, John Bunting, and Steve Zabel, not only held the Cowboys to ten points, but Bergey landed a vicious tackle on Cowboys running back Doug Dennison, causing a fumble. Defensive back Joe Lavender scooped up the fumble and returned it ninety-six yards for a touchdown.

With the score tied at 10, we were facing fourth-and-three at the Cowboys thirty-eight, with five seconds left on the clock.

Tom Dempsey was not your average kicker. There was no one else like him in the NFL. Born with only half a right hand and half a right foot, Tom was one of the larger personalities on the team. Topping 6'3" and 260 plus pounds, he earned the nickname "Big Demps" from his Eagles teammate Bill Bradley, who occasionally sang it to the tune of Jimmy Dean's hit, *Big John*.

The Cowboys called a time-out to "ice" Dempsey, but nothing bothered the NFL record-holder for the longest field goal. While he was with the New Orleans Saints in 1970, he had kicked a record-setting sixty-three-yard field goal to beat the Detroit Lions.

In the huddle, Dempsey looked at each of us and shouted, "Get your man and I'll make this kick!" As the outside linebacker, I had a tough assignment for field goals. My mission was to block my rusher to the inside and then bounce out and chip block the weakest rusher to protect the kick from being blocked.

Tension was high on both sides. As soon as the ball was snapped, I got the inside Cowboy and got just enough of the outside rusher to keep him wide. I hit the ground following the second block. Then I heard the solid thump of Dempsey's foot striking the football. As we lay on the turf, we watched it sail through the uprights for the game winning score.

The Eagles won 13–10, finally stopping the eleven-game, seven-year drought of losing against the Dallas Cowboys. And it happened on *Monday Night Football*. It didn't get any better than that for this homegrown Eagle, #52! I was twenty-three and playing for the team that I had rooted for every week since the 1960s at Franklin Field.

It was more than just a dream come true—it surpassed *all* my dreams. I figured there was nowhere to go but up with the rejuvenated Eagles.

The Dallas victory put the Eagles into the win column. We were now 1–1 starting the 1974 season. Our newfound confidence propelled the Eagles to a four-game winning streak as we beat our next three rivals. As the only NFC East team with a 4–1 record, the team and fans began dreaming about a potential Super Bowl run.

But it was not meant to be. On October 20, on the return visit to Dallas, another street fight battle ensued and "Roger the Dodger" Staubach brought the Cowboys back in the fourth quarter to steal a 31–24 win. In an instant, the wind went out from under the Eagles wings. Our team spiraled down with five straight losses. A three-game winning streak at the end of the season resulted in a 7–7 record and cautious optimism going into 1975.

Unfortunately, my run as #52 in Eagles green would be cut short in 1975. In the fourth of six pre-season games, I suffered a knee injury while making a tackle on a punt return. As I tackled the ball carrier, we tangled with the referee and chains that mark the downs during the game. I fell awkwardly and twisted my knee badly. Fortunately, nothing was torn, but I stretched out the ligaments enough to be put on injured reserve. On November 13, the same day I was taken off injured reserve, I was claimed on waivers by the New England Patriots. I played the final five games of the 1975 season with the Pats.

Soon after joining New England, outside linebacker Steve King was injured and I had the opportunity to start my first two NFL games. Not only did I play the entire game at linebacker, I was also in the game on special teams. In our game against the Jets, I twice tackled All-Pro fullback John Riggins and was credited with a goal line sack on the legendary Joe Namath. I suspect that the extra drama I added rising slowly from Namath's legs, aided in my receiving the credit from the game's official statisticians.

In my second and last game as a starter against the Buffalo Bills, I tackled the NFL rushing record-holder, O.J. Simpson. Of course, I had a couple of serious misses too, but in that regard, I was not the only one who missed him that day. Early in that game, I had my greatest NFL moment when I intercepted a Joe Ferguson pass at our own ten-yard line and ran like hell down the sideline to the end zone for the score. As I rose-up to punt the ball into the Buffalo stands (something I always planned to do if I ever scored), I was smothered by my friend Steve Zabel as I struggled for oxygen. Some of my euphoria was short circuited when I saw the red flag and the ball was called back to the forty-five, where an offending Eagle clip was thrown. I lost the score but was credited with an interception and a forty-five-yard return.

CHAPTER 13

|||||||||||||||||||||||||||||||||||||||||||||||||||||||||||||||||||||||||||||||||||||||||||

Planning the Great Escape

New York, 1979

"If you continue to improve like this, maybe we can release you on Wednesday."

Back in the hospital the morning after my night out with John and Renee, I woke up around 6:00 AM. There was always a rise in hallway noise during the changing of the hospital guard. The autumn sunrise was also slowly creeping into the room.

My plan that day was to eat all my meals, do several laps around the fifteenth-floor hallways, get my temperature under a hundred degrees, and go to the bathroom by myself. Small actions I had always taken for granted when I had been a healthy athlete. Now, they were the key to freedom.

If I accomplished all four of those tasks, then day eight would be getaway day, according to what Dr. Marcove had told me a few days earlier. I was sure he had said, "If you continue to improve like this, maybe we can release you on Wednesday." That was tomorrow! It was the only thing I could concentrate on.

I promptly got to work, forcing down my breakfast of cold scrambled eggs, yogurt, a small fruit cup, two pieces of white toast, and a warm glass of orange juice. One meal down, two more to go. My temperature was a little high that morning, spiking at 101.5 degrees, but I reassured myself I had a busy night and overextended it a bit.

It was like being in training camp all over again. I had my bandages redressed, made a few phone calls and threw down two pain pills. It was time for me to set a new lap record around the fifteenth-floor hallway. My goal that morning was ten laps. Based on last night's walk around New York, I was confident that ten laps would not be a problem. I was so buoyed with the thought of going home that I blew my record away with a twelve-lap performance. In the process, my temperature had risen to 102, so I flushed down fluids and rested to calm myself down.

I could tell I was reaching my breaking point. I wanted to be home now. Not even tomorrow, but that very instant. It had gotten to be too much. The thought of another night of interruptions from nurses checking my temperature and hearing the intermittent moans and cries from other patients was making me ill. The sterile smell of the hospital itself seemed stuck in my sinus cavity. Even today, I can still close my eyes and smell the medicinal odors that Sloan Kettering emitted day and night.

I wanted to be in my own bed surrounded by my wife and three children, safe in the knowledge that my extended family was only a phone call away. Most of all, I wanted to get back into my old routine of going to work each day, exercising again and finding out for myself what I could and couldn't do as a four-quarter amputee.

When my lunch arrived at noon that day the cheerful nurse said, "Make sure you eat it all." I grimaced but complied. In less than twenty-two hours, I would be out the door. At least, that's what Doc said, didn't he? And I know he meant it because he said that I was no ordinary patient who needed the usual two weeks to recover from this kind of operation. I said to myself, he would never tell me that I could go home in eight days unless he meant it.

I successfully completed all my goals for day seven, although my temperature was still hovering around 101. I was sure a good night's sleep would fix the problem. As I drifted off to sleep that night, all that I could think of was going home in the morning. I was excited to see my family and my home and very happy to be alive. I just couldn't wait until morning.

My last phone call of the evening was to my dad, who planned to leave Wilmington at 7:00 AM with Dave Jenkins, a buddy from Xerox. We estimated that they would arrive around 9:30 for the 110-mile trip out of Manhattan and back to Delaware. I looked over at the clock on the wall. It was now 10:30 PM. In less than twelve hours, I would be home.

||||||||||||||||||||||||||||||||||||||||||||||||||||||||||||||||||||||||||||||||||||||||||||||||||||

Patriot Days

Smithfield, Rhode Island., July 4, 1976

**"I loved playing in the National Football League,
but hated the NFL training camps."**

O ur nation's 200th birthday was a major cause of celebration
for the country. For me, it was memorable for another
reason. It was my last day at home before reporting to
the New England Patriots' training camp at Bryant College in
Smithfield, Rhode Island.

I loved playing in the National Football League, but I hated the
NFL training camps—ten weeks of extreme physical exertion,
including two full-scale scrimmages and six pre-season games.
I could expect to lose ten to twelve pounds during those twice-
daily practices. These sessions would last more than two hours
each, morning and evening in summer heat averaging eighty-five
to ninety-five degrees. Each night, before lights out at 10:00, we
all prayed for rain or at least some cloud cover.

I always felt a certain separation anxiety when heading out of
town, but this time the homeward pull was even greater. My wife
Cathy was pregnant with our first child, a son we would name
Brett. Also, I was not in a good mental state for the 1976 season
for several reasons. First, I was starting a family. As I had already

learned, the NFL could trade you to another team in another city, giving you only twenty-four hours to report to the new team. That process could put major stress on family life by keeping a father hundreds of miles from his family, which couldn't just pick up and move at a moment's notice.

Secondly, it was clear to me that the Patriots did not have me in their future plans. I was basically their insurance in case someone got hurt in the pre-season. And lastly, my left shoulder was hurting. I assumed it was from the pounding I took playing special teams for the Eagles in 1974 and 1975.

In the early morning of July 5, my dad drove me to the Philadelphia airport for my flight to ten weeks in the cauldron.

I must say my spirits rose when I got to Bryant College and was reunited with linebackers Steve Zabel, Steve Nelson, Sam Hunt, and Steve King, as well as quarterbacks Jim Plunkett and Steve Grogan. I really liked the guys on this football team. They made me feel welcome when I joined the team mid-season the previous year after being released by the Eagles.

Kevin with fellow linebacker Steve Zabel

New England also presented, by far, the best weather I had ever experienced in any summer camp since my high school days at Salesianum. It was consistently around eighty degrees with very low humidity, so you didn't feel completely drained following the afternoon practice.

Hitting on this Chuck Fairbanks' team was another issue. Fairbanks was new to the NFL following a successful coaching career at the college level at the University of Oklahoma. With well over a hundred players on his college roster each year, he didn't have to worry as much about injuries or depth. If someone got hurt at OU, there was always someone waiting in the wings to take his position. He also knew he was only getting three or four years with each player, regardless of their talent, due to the abbreviated time span of college. This wasn't the case in the NFL. In professional football, quality players were at a premium.

It took Fairbanks two pre-seasons to figure out that you couldn't carry out full-on hitting sessions for an hour at every practice without expecting injuries. Unfortunately, this was still the year he conducted daily full-contact sessions.

This was also the point in time that I realized that in addition to the pain in my left shoulder, it was also noticeably weaker than my right. It was evident during one-on-one blocking and shedding drills against the tight ends the linebackers fought against during every practice, scrimmage or game. I hoped it was just battle wounds that would recover in time.

After one pre-season game where I played only two series on defense, I was released on waivers. I returned home to Delaware and decided to take time off to get bigger, healthier and stronger. The three seasons I had played linebacker and special teams had obviously taken a toll on my body.

||||||||||||||||||||||||||||||||||||||||||||||||||||||||||||||||||||||||||||||||||

CHAPTER 15

The Discharge Crisis

New York, eight days after surgery

"And you would, wouldn't you, Mr. Tough Guy."

The morning I was to be released, I woke up a little before 6:00 AM raring to go. By 8:30, I was packed, showered, dressed, had breakfast and my temperature taken. It was 99.5 degrees. The only thing left to do was have Dr. Marcove check me out and sign my release papers.

I thought I looked fairly normal as I checked myself out in the bathroom mirror. I had strapped on the temporary prosthetic shoulder that a volunteer had sewn for me. I wore a button-down shirt under a dark blue blazer.

With my recent weight loss and the absence of intense pain that was constantly etched in my face prior to the operation, I believe I actually looked healthier than I had looked in over a year.

I began to feel the effects of that morning's pain pills. Not only did they alleviate the throbbing pain of a hundred stitches that were eight days old, they kept me from becoming too anxious about getting home to my wife and family. By then, I had been at the hospital for so long I was on my third new roommate.

"Nice to meet you," I said to the new guy, but I kept it brief. He would soon get his own new roommate, so it didn't seem to make sense to take the time to learn each other's stories.

At 9:00 AM, Joan walked into my room but didn't look happy. "I've got some disappointing news for you," she said. "Dr. Marcove won't be coming in today."

I couldn't believe it.

Then she added, "You might not be released until Saturday."

I asked her if she was kidding. My voice rose as I said, "I'll miss your sense of humor, Joan, but not this hospital."

For a brief second, I held onto the hope that she was just teasing me, since she knew more than anyone how impatient I was to get home. But she wasn't smiling. Joan tried to convince me with a soothing tone that three days wasn't the end of the world and might even be beneficial.

She might as well have said three more months. "Where is he?" I demanded.

Joan explained that Marcove was at Orthopedic Institute down the street performing an emergency operation and would be tied up all day.

I had already mentally left this hospital around 8:30, and I wasn't coming back for anyone. I began pacing. Sweat trickled down my neck and my throat started to close. I think I was experiencing a full-blown anxiety attack.

Darting out into the hallway, I walked rapidly around the corridor and weighed my options. My dad and Dave would arrive any minute, and I felt fine to go home. What the hell was the matter with Marcove? He promised he would release me. Could someone else release me? What if I just walked out the door? They couldn't hold me. But would it upset the Doc so much that he would drop me as a patient? This just wasn't fair.

I went back to the room and picked up the phone to call my mother at home. My new roommate, who was around sixty and a definite New Yorker, looked at me as if I was a mental patient instead of a cancer patient. My mother did her best to calm me down and suggested I say some prayers and just wait until they got there.

"It'll all work out," she told me. I hung up the phone and reached for a towel to wipe the sweat off my face.

Joan came in and handed me a small piece of paper with a phone number on it. "Dr. Marcove is in pre-op right now. This is the phone number of the room he is in. You didn't get this from me." And she fled the room and the upcoming scene.

A nurse answered and I said, "Can I speak to Dr. Marcove? It's a bit of an emergency."

"Who is this?" she asked.

"Dr. Reilly," I replied. There wasn't anything I wouldn't do to be released today. If it helped, I would have done the operation for him. After a long pause, I heard a very annoyed Ralph Marcove get on the line. "Yes, what is it?" he demanded.

"You told me you were going to release me today, and I'm all set to go," I told him. "Could you make that happen?"

There was an audible sigh and then, "Listen, Kevin, your surgery took almost half a day. Your body has been through enormous trauma and you need more rest before I release you. I have never released anyone this soon. Ever."

"Just relax, Doc," I said. "I promise I'll be in first thing Saturday morning. You can take out the stitches, talk next steps, and everything will be right on schedule."

"That isn't protocol."

"Wait a minute, Doc," I pleaded. "You said I could leave today if I continued to improve. You haven't even been in to see how well I'm doing."

He wasn't responding. "You know what, Doc?" I yelled impatiently. "This isn't a prison. Have you ever had a patient leave on you before being released, because I'm about to do it? I hope it doesn't piss you off to the point where you refuse to be my doctor going forward, but all I can tell you is that if I stay here one more hour, I'm going to lose it. And you don't want that to happen."

I didn't hear anything for a while when he mumbled something along the lines of, "And you would, wouldn't you, Mr. Tough Guy?"

In a disapproving tone, Dr. Marcove told me, "It's against my better judgment." He paused to sigh once more. "Put nurse Kaiser on the phone. I'm sure she's there."

Joan had returned to the room so I sheepishly handed her the phone. He first chewed her out for giving me the number before giving her explicit instructions about getting me released.

Joan then handed me back the phone, whispering, "I don't know who he's angrier at, you or me."

Dr. Marcove once again told me that against his better judgment he was going to have me officially released. He also stressed that I would be sorry because it was too soon. I thanked him profusely and apologized for creating a scene.

I promised that I would be back in a week for a checkup, to which he replied, "I don't want you on any highway for two weeks. You'll soon find out what I'm talking about."

I didn't care about anything but getting out of there. By this time is was a little past 9:30. Right on schedule, my father and Dave arrived. "Ready to go?" my dad asked as they walked into the room. "Why are you sweating so bad?" Dave asked. "Your shirt is soaking wet!"

I told them that I would explain later as I quickly changed into a dry shirt. Within a half an hour, I had my meds, more bandages and instructions for a week. I gave Joan a big, one-arm hug. She had been my rock through some of the most difficult moments of my life.

We headed to the elevator and my escape. My dad's car was parked at the entrance to the hospital. As I made my way to the car, the brisk October air dried the remaining sweat from my brow. I felt the sense of new beginnings that autumn always brought to me, just like it had as a boy for each new school year and football season.

After the relative quiet of the hospital, I felt the pulse and sounds of the city in motion: people talking, taxi horns blowing, and car doors slamming. The bright sun shone as if to welcome me back to the real world. As I climbed into the back seat of my dad's Chevy Impala, I thought about how lucky I was to be leaving the hospital alive.

As we pulled onto the New Jersey Turnpike that day, I couldn't stop talking. I jabbered like an excited teenager about that morning's drama and my ultimate escape. About an hour into the drive, I felt exhausted. My body was completely drained. Was it the drugs kicking in, all the excitement or both? I had to lie down in the backseat because I was going downhill quickly and we still had another hour or so to go.

By the time we pulled up to my house, I was giving one-word answers and wondering if I could make it into the house on my own two feet. Nausea also overwhelmed me. I pushed to make it the thirty steps from the car to the living room. As I plopped down on the couch, exhausted and dizzy, I thought about Marcove's warning about the trauma my body had been through.

For the next three days, I did little other than eat, sleep, and take my meds. I could go short spurts at maybe seventy percent, but the longer I was up, the slower everything about me became. Exhaustion came quickly and easily. It was a very humbling experience. For once in my life, I decided to surrender to the slow healing process and stop fighting it. The doc had been right. Oh, he had been so right!

‖‖

CHAPTER 16

A Job in the Real World

Wilmington, Delaware, 1976

"He's bringing me in for an interview tomorrow
at 8:30. Can you believe that?"

By November 1976, despite the shoulder concerns, I was feeling much better. I had built myself back into playing shape but there was not a single call to re-join the NFL. It was becoming increasingly clear that I would sit out the entire season. My next best chance for returning to the NFL would be to sign as a free agent in the spring and go through a 1977 training camp with a team that was thin at linebacker or needed an experienced special team player and back-up long snapper.

However, that potential opportunity was months away, and I had to start thinking about getting a real job with a company that would hire me knowing that I might play another year or two of professional football. This would require an arrangement where they would allow me to work during the off season with the idea that I could return to full-time at the end of my playing days.

Meanwhile, I was able to work part-time in my dad's liquor store, putting a few dollars in my pocket while keeping up my workout regimen. Then I had one of those fateful experiences that make you believe there is indeed "divine intervention."

It was a weekday morning just before the store opened at 9:00 AM, and I was discussing my job prospects with my dad. He strongly advised me to get into a sales position with a respectable corporation like IBM. While we were talking, a loud screech occurred outside the store on Route 202, the main artery between Wilmington and West Chester, Pennsylvania.

A flatbed truck had skidded to a halt at the traffic light and a full load of plywood had shifted. About twenty large sheets of plywood had slid off the truck, scattering into the right-hand lane next to the truck. The truck driver, who stood no more than about 5'5" with a slim build, got out of the truck and threw up his hands in the air in disgust. "Why don't you go out there and help that guy reload his truck before there's an accident," my dad said. "I'll watch the store."

I went out and told the trucker to get on the back of the truck, and I would throw the sheets of plywood up so he could restack them and tie them down. I had worked for two years with a home builder during the summer, and I had gotten pretty good at tossing heavy plywood to the guys who were nailing them down to the roof rafters.

While I was on the street tossing up the plywood, a former Delaware State football player, who once had a tryout with the Eagles, was filling his car at the service station adjacent to the liquor store. Although I knew all about John Land, we had never met. He recognized me.

While not a household name, John Land was well known in the football world. In fact, during the first year of the World Football League, he finished third in rushing with over a thousand yards and sixth in receiving. In an effort to compete with the NFL, the fledgling league had lured away big-name players such as

Miami Dolphin stars Larry Csonka and Jim Kiick, plus Dallas star Calvin Hill, among others.

John played for the Philadelphia Bell, coached by Delaware football legend and former NFL Pro Bowl selection Ron Waller. The team included other area favorites like Vince Papale, Ron Holliday, and King Corcoran. Waller, the old coach who knew football as well as anyone had once said, "The only back I would ever choose ahead of John Land to run a football for me would be O.J. Simpson."

Waller had also recruited John when he was coaching with the Eagles minor league affiliate, the Pottstown Firebirds. John was in pre-season camp with the Baltimore Colts when he received

the call. He was offered $1,000 a game. All he had to do was show up and run the ball. He would not even have to practice with the team. As a young husband with a baby on the way, John took Waller and the Firebirds up on the offer and left the Colts.

John Land on a sweep

Today, people look at the big money in pro sports and often do not realize that most NFL players at that time still needed to work in the off season to make ends meet. While John ran a football for Pottstown, he also had a full-time position at the Ferris School for delinquent boys in Wilmington. With a chance to join the sales force of a Fortune 100 company, John settled down into his post football life. Fortunately for me, he happened to have stopped for gas that day next to Van's Liquors and knew a 235-pound linebacker when he saw one.

As I was walking back to the store, I was intercepted by John looking rather dapper decked out in a blue pin striped suit. "Hi, Kevin," he said extending his hand. "I'm John Land." Smiles broke out on both our faces and we gave each other the NFL shoulder hug while still shaking hands.

John proceeded to tell me that his football career was officially over and he had joined the sales force at Xerox. He had been on the job six months and felt it was an outstanding company. I asked him if they were still hiring. He said that there was a pause in hiring, but the company was growing rapidly and he was sure there would soon be more opportunities. In another stroke of luck, he mentioned that his boss and hiring manager, Dick Keely, was a proud Villanova alumnus and it wouldn't hurt to give him a call.

After parting ways with John, I headed back into the liquor store to tell my dad, struck by the irony that we were just discussing corporate sales before the truck incident. On my break at 10:30, I gave Dick Keely a call, and we talked for fifteen minutes. After I hung up, my dad asked, "How did it go?"

"He's bringing me in for an interview tomorrow at 8:30. Can you believe that?"

At 10:00 AM the next morning, I signed an offer letter to become an employee for one the top companies and brands in the business world. Little did I know that I would spend my next thirty years with the company.

Relieved to have a full-time job in the corporate world, I still considered it a back-up plan for my NFL ambitions. But the small bump in my shoulder began to grow and I would soon face my first surgery to remove it. Not too long after that, I would be visiting Sloan Kettering to meet Dr. Marcove.

CHAPTER 17

The Road to Recovery

Wilmington, Delaware, 1979

"Hey Doc, I need another prescription for pain pills. I'm almost out."

In addition to the trauma of the surgery and shock to my body, I had never gone this long in my life without being physically active. So, when I stepped out of the car after the 120-mile ride following the escape from Sloan Kettering, I felt more drained than from any NFL two-a-day practice that I had ever experienced.

The strain of the morning and my lack of stamina had seriously depleted my resources. This was on top of the emotional rollercoaster of walking into my house to see my family for the first time since the surgery—a surgery I was not sure I would survive, a surgery that had dramatically altered my physical appearance and my future.

Fortunately, my children were so young at the time that they did not realize I was so different. They were just happy to see me. After a quick bite to eat, I collapsed into bed. I was asleep the second my head hit the pillow and didn't wake up for sixteen hours.

Where was I? What time was it? What day was it? Had I actually slept nearly sixteen hours without even a bathroom break?

Dr. Marcove had tried to explain how weak my body was, but I had trouble absorbing what that meant. As I sat there in the bedroom thinking, it suddenly dawned on me that the road to recovery was going to be more of an uphill battle than I had ever anticipated. It would surely dwarf any challenge that I had previously encountered in twenty-nine years, including those four NFL training camps. Recovery was going to be a different kind of challenge.

Rocky Bleier had warned me: "There ain't a whole lot of instruction to these sort of comebacks; it's mostly trial and error."

I wobbled down the stairs to our family room, looking for the kids to get a hug. I could not believe how wiped out I still felt after such a long sleep. The strange and painful sensation I was warned about, the "phantom sensation" was attacking my mind and body. It felt like the arm and shoulder were still there but with what I can only describe as "pins and needles." It was really getting on my nerves. It never seemed to go away and only diminished when I took the pain medication.

My first three days home from the hospital became somewhat of a blur because I was sleeping more than twelve hours a day, perhaps resting overtime in order to heal the gigantic wound. I repeatedly looked in the mirror at the empty space and stitches that extended over the customized resin plate that now replaced my entire left shoulder—the only thing protecting my left lung and heart.

Thank heavens none of the desmoid tumor had invaded the chest cavity that contained my vital organs. At least in one respect, I had dodged a desmoid bullet.

On the fifth day, a group of my best friends came over for a brief visit. They were well aware of the rest orders I was under. Larry and Cathy Pietropaulo, Tony and Joyce Nerlinger, and Phil and Eileen Leach were welcome faces. For the first time in weeks, I was in a better frame of mind.

Just when I was starting to have a little fun and relax, Cathy reminded them again of my doctor's rest orders, and we walked them to their cars. It was early evening, and they were going to go out for drinks. I wanted to go in the worst way. I wanted to pick up right where I left off in my life as husband, father, and friend. We could be normal, going out on this cool November evening with the smell of smoke from recently lit fireplaces. A night with friends could be just the elixir I thought I needed to start picking up the pieces in my life.

The sad reality was that I wouldn't have lasted an hour at a bar or restaurant before the heavy eyelids and phantom sensation would have overtaken me and I would have had to limp on home to bed.

Cathy and I wandered back to the house after saying goodbye. A sudden melancholy engulfed me. As great as it was to see my friends, it was apparent that the group treated me differently. I could sense an attitude of "poor Kev." I was a former football star now struggling as an amputee with three young children, an uncertain medical prognosis, and at best a cloudy career and life prospects.

I know my situation hit my buddy Larry hard. I saw it in his eyes. His empathy did nothing to bolster my confidence. I sat in my family room with sadness and a new reality coming down on me like the darkness of the November night.

When Cathy excused herself to go to bed, I decided to stay up awhile longer, well rested from two days of near coma-like sleep to ponder my new reality. As I stoked the fire in the solitude of the family room, alone with my thoughts, I can honestly say that I was now more afraid than ever as to what might lie ahead for the new one-arm man.

I was particularly concerned about the monthly appointments I needed over the next year to check on a possible reoccurrence of the tumor. I was deeply affected by the reality that I would not be deemed to be in remission from the desmoid disease for ten years.

I was also beginning to focus on the physical limitations that I had not fully anticipated, but that I knew lay ahead. Would I be able to drive a car? Dress myself? Button buttons, zip zippers, or tie shoes? What about woodworking, home repair, golf, racquetball, swimming, weightlifting, fishing, and so on? I wasn't sure if I would be able to do any of them.

Hell, I was only twenty-nine years old. Just four years before, I weighed a strapping 235 pounds, had a 375-pound bench press, started a couple games for the New England Patriots, and had tackled the likes of O.J. Simpson, John Riggins, and Franco Harris. Now I was significantly disabled and deeply discouraged.

My mind raced as the fire crackled, and the phantom pain continued to scream at me. I knew I wasn't dreaming and that I had to come to some form of acceptance right then and there. So, I did the only thing that anyone can do in these times of seeming despair. I prayed.

I got down on my knees in the room that night and prayed like I never prayed before. I wanted to live. I wanted to see my children grow and my family to be happy and not scarred by my situation. I wanted to work again. I wanted to be useful and be a success despite my disability. I wanted my old normal life back, just like it was with my family and friends and hobbies and projects.

"God, dear God," I prayed. "If you answer my prayers, I promise I'll give back to others and never complain again. I promise. You'll see a new Kevin Reilly."

It's funny, looking back from today and thinking that was the way God works. You have a big wakeup call with a crisis, a change of heart and perspective, offer some neat and simple negotiations sealed with a verbal promise, and then you're ready to roll.

With more than sixteen years of Catholic education under my belt, that was simply how I thought. And believe it or not, that little talk with the Man upstairs helped me tremendously that night. As a matter of fact, I remember my closing words, "God if you help me with these requests, I'll reset my life's goals and be all I can be and more. You have my commitment."

While the prayer that night helped me briefly reset my attitude, it didn't take long for new doubts and anxiety to creep back in. My brain was becoming overwhelmed in anticipation of the trip back to New York and my check-up appointment with Dr. Marcove.

Each day the tension rose to a new level and before I knew it, my father and I were making the two-and-a-half-hour trek back to Sloan Kettering. My stomach was in knots, and my anxiety level was a nine on a scale of ten.

As we exited the Lincoln Tunnel onto 42nd Street to the hustle and bustle of a weekday Manhattan morning, I was worried sick that Dr. Marcove would find a reason to put me back in the hospital. I worried that the skin that was pulled over the resin plate was not getting enough blood and that it might not be healing properly, or that they had discovered more desmoid in one of the tissues they had biopsied near my neck area. Like a chorus in a song, Marcove's statement, "I think I got it all" kept playing over and over in my mind.

After only thirty minutes amongst the sad humanity in the waiting room, Marcove appeared and we moved to the examination room. As he began to probe my stitches for any signs of infection, I held my breath. He moved to my neck area where he seemed to have some concern. My heart pounded so hard that I felt it in my temples.

Finally, he spoke. "Everything looks good."

Talk about relief! I could feel all the tension release from my body.

Marcove then started to remove the stitches one-by-one with scissors but quickly seemed to lose interest. He looked at me and said, "Your sister is a nurse, right?" I barely got out a yes before he said, "Good. She can take the rest of the stitches out. I don't have the time. See you in six weeks, big guy."

"Sounds good to me, Doc," I blurted out, relieved beyond description. As he was getting ready to leave, I suddenly remembered something important. "Hey Doc, I need another prescription for pain pills. I'm almost out."

Marcove turned to me and looked me straight in the eye. "Aspirin from now on, big guy," he said. "It's time to get off the pain meds."

"But Doc, with this constant phantom sensation, that's the only way I can get to sleep."

"If the pain is bothering you that much, I can put you back in the hospital," he said. "I didn't cure you from one disease to lose you to another."

That was the end of the conversation and the beginning of the long road back. The poor Kevin pity party was officially over. It was time to dig deep—mentally, physically, and spiritually and get back into the game. I knew hard work lay ahead of me and I would have to "man up" if I was going to make it.

PART II

Faith, Family, Friends, and Fortitude

*In the surf at Stone Harbor
with daughter Erin, 1980*

Author's Note:

When Rocky Bleier counseled me after my surgery to never give up on anything until I had tried it at least three times, I took it to heart. I wanted to do many of the things in "the life after" that I had before and wanted to pursue as much of my life bucket list as possible. But I would soon find out that nothing in life is a straight line. There continued to be mountains to climb and serious detours along the way, especially the divorce that I never saw coming. And for many years after the surgery, I not only had to adapt to the obvious issue of having one arm, I had to deal with "phantom pain" and dread that the desmoid tumor might return at any time.

By condensing the events of my life into Part II of this book, it may seem that my life was rather frenetic and unfocused, particularly in the early years following the surgery. I was doing all I could to keep my mind off my health issues. Many of the things I got involved with, in addition to my day job, including public speaking and broadcasting to charity work and sports management, were in many respects an extension of my values and my interests. In time, however, I would find that my most rewarding activity was the time I committed to helping others. For several reasons—not the least of which is my status as an amputee, people regularly sought me out to for advice and counsel when facing amputation, cancer, or addiction.

So, fasten your seatbelt for a wild ride with the one-armed man. You will meet some amazing people and familiar names along the way. I hope you enjoy my long and continuing recovery story.

CHAPTER 18

Back to Work

"That's crazy, but I swear I just saw Kevin Reilly go past the window dangling from a parasail."

In 1979, there were very few rehabilitation facilities for amputees, so the fact that no one recommended or referred me for therapy or training did not really phase me. I gave it little thought and just assumed that I would learn as I always had, by the school of hard knocks and repetition. The only help that I expected was to be fitted for a prosthetic shoulder after my scars healed. The shoulder was to be simply a cosmetic device designed to square off my left side to match my right so that shirts and jackets would be evenly matched, thereby minimizing the appearance of the forequarter amputation. It would look like I was only missing my left arm.

During my early fog of recovery and depression, I never thought that there was a positive side to my situation. I soon realized one significant blessing: I had lost my non-dominant arm.

Because I was right handed, I would not have to re-learn some of the most normal and basic daily activities, such as writing, steering, brushing my teeth, eating with a spoon or fork, combing my hair, throwing a ball, shaking hands, and buttoning a shirt, just to name a few. Even things that I soon trained myself to do one handed, such as tying my necktie, tying my shoes, splitting firewood, pushing a lawnmower or snow blower, sawing a board or hammering a nail, were all possible due to the existing dexterity and coordination present in my right arm.

As my balance and stamina began to return, I was able to resume certain physical activities, such as racquetball. It was great to be back on the court where I could compete and get a great workout playing only two months after my operation. I also did not have to endure the frustration of relearning the mechanics of the game from the other side. I had great satisfaction of competing against, and even beating at times, my two-armed opponents.

In January of 1980, after eight weeks of being out on disability, I went back to work full-time. My doctor and family thought it was too soon, but I was bored sitting at home. I wanted to start the new year off back in my sales position with Xerox. I wanted to show everyone that I was back and ready to pick up where I left off, striving to be among the best performers in the company. To their credit, Xerox's management team welcomed me back with open arms. But there would be no easing into it. I would be expected to manage hundreds of accounts, solve everyday customer problems and meet all my sales targets beginning with the very first month.

After a successful January, in which I wore myself out physically and mentally, I drifted into a funk that had me struggling to get out of bed in the morning. I felt exhausted to the point where I quickly forgot about the benefit of losing my non-dominant arm versus my right arm. Leading the chorus of negative thoughts that seemed to blast through my brain every hour was the almost paralyzing thought of my next doctor's appointment with the possibility of the desmoid tumor returning.

Maybe it was inevitable, but soon my old linebacker mentality started to return or perhaps it was a growing "live for today" attitude. I often found myself crashing ahead with a certain reckless abandon, figuring I may not have that long to live.

That April, after just three months back on the job, Cathy and I attended the annual Xerox sales recognition trip to Acapulco, Mexico. The company was kind enough to include me, although I was not technically eligible since I was not in a sales territory for all of 1979. While figuring out our flight arrangements for the trip, one of my colleagues joked, "I want to be on Kevin's flight because there's little chance of a crash. Nothing else could ever happen to him!"

As soon as we arrived at our Acapulco hotel, I noticed a parasail in the sky. My "live for today" impulse suddenly kicked in, and I dropped our bags and headed to the beach wondering if I could fit into one of those parachute harnesses. Two locals who couldn't speak a word of English but who obviously understood P.T. Barnum's famous line that "there's a sucker born every minute" were all too willing to try to fit the man with no arm or shoulder into what passed for a harness for $150. As they struggled to figure it out, one of them accidentally raised his arm so that the guy in the speedboat sitting 100 yards offshore thought it was the go signal. The next thing I know is I am being dragged along the water, half in and half out of the harness and suddenly airborne and hanging on for dear life.

In his room on the twentieth floor of the hotel, one of our executives, Bob Berman turned to his wife and said, "That's crazy, but I swear I just saw Kevin Reilly go past the window dangling from a parasail."

Team Xerox at my daughter Erin's wedding, 2001. Joe Teti, Dave Jenkins, Tom Pitts, Brett Reilly, Bob Souffie, Kevin Reilly, and John Riley

||||||||||||||||||||||||||||||||||||||||||||||||||||||||||||||||||||||||||||||||||||||||||||||||||||

CHAPTER 19

Scrimmage Line Nights

"Call 'em as you see 'em."

In the year following my surgery, life began to stabilize and I fell into a routine with work. Cathy went back to teaching and playing her banjo in her father's band. As Miss Delaware, she had won the talent portion of the Miss America Pageant in 1975.

The kids were now attending pre-school, and soon I would be helping to coach them in T-ball and basketball. However, Dad did look a little different than the other fathers. The one thing that took some getting used to were the quick double takes from anyone when they first noticed me and the prolonged stares from kids. This was often followed by, "Hey, Mister, what happened to your arm?" This situation continues to the present day, but more on that later.

One aspect of my life that was unaffected by my health challenge and amputation was my ability to think on my feet and talk sports from behind a microphone. During my first year with the Eagles and well before starting at Xerox, I had an opportunity to do some sports broadcasting. I would have to say it was love at first sight—or, should I say, first word.

My first opportunity at sports broadcasting came courtesy of the dean of Delaware sportscasters, Bill Pheiffer. Bill was the sports director for Delaware's number one radio station, WDEL 1150AM. I had known Bill since my football days at Salesianum.

Bill was a Navy veteran of WWII, having served as a gunner on a torpedo bomber. After the war, he graduated in 1949 from Lafayette College and began a career in television and radio. In addition to his daily radio broadcasts, Bill provided play-by-play for University of Delaware football, basketball, and baseball games for over thirty years. He had a stint as the television play-by-play announcer for the NBA's Philadelphia Warriors, Philadelphia "Big Five" basketball, and the Wilmington Blue Bombers' semi-pro basketball team. Bill was also the voice of Salesianum football for twenty-five years. A handsome guy with a classic radio voice, Bill had all the ingredients for a career on the national level, but due to bad timing and circumstances beyond his control, he missed out on several chances.

So, when Pie, as his close friends called him, asked if I would like to be a guest on his Monday night sports call-in program, I jumped at the chance. The call-in show was a new format at that time but has now evolved into a major part of our sports culture. The host is very reliant on getting phone calls from listeners to fill the two-hour broadcast time, and Bill was having trouble getting calls, sometimes going twenty to thirty minutes between them. By having me as a guest, he could eliminate the long monologues and have someone to talk to between calls.

I guess due to being the local kid who played for the beloved Philadelphia Eagles, the phone rang off the hook that night. Callers wanted the inside story on the new Eagles team that was now going to be led by outstanding middle linebacker Bill Bergey on defense and former league MVP Roman Gabriel at quarterback. After the show, Bill asked if there was any way I could be a guest the following week. I not only came back the next week, I ended up being a guest each Monday night for the rest of 1973.

What I learned as a twenty-two-year-old, wet behind the ears broadcaster from the "Velvet Tongue Devil" Bill Pheiffer was probably the equivalent of a twelve-credit semester at any broadcast school. After every show, he gave me tips and constructive criticism. He showed me how to work the electronic radio board and microphone levels, how to take and close out telephone calls, and how to record public service announcements and commercials. Pie also invited me to join him to do play-by-play for high school football. But the number one thing he taught me was "call 'em as you see 'em," trust your experience and knowledge, and be sure to always do your homework.

I really enjoyed my time in the studio, so during my playing career and after, I took every opportunity I could to work with Bill and WDEL. Not only did it fit well with my work schedule, it increased my name recognition and led to broader community exposure. This helped to open doors in the sales world and created speaking opportunities.

Following my amputation surgery and Bill Bergey's retirement from football, we joined together at WDEL on a two-hour sports program, called *Scrimmage Line*. Similar to my experience with Bill Pheiffer's call-in sports show, we huddled in the WDEL studio and waited for the calls to pour in. But just like Pheiffer's show, we were very reliant on the phones ringing and that did not always happen.

Bergey had previously been a guest on WIP Philadelphia's sports call-in program that was held at a local tavern. He suggested that we give the "remote" format a try. The concept of the sports bar with lots of big screen TVs was evolving. The only one in the area, Stanley's Tavern, was just down the road from the studio.

Stanley's was owned by Bill and my dentist, Howdy Giles, and managed by our friend Steve Torpey. They loved the idea of broadcasting from their bar and a deal was quickly struck.

At Stanley's with Bergey, Don Voltz and Bill Werndel

At that time, *Monday Night Football* with Howard Cosell, Frank Gifford, and Don Meredith was at the top of the ratings. We set up on site at Stanley's and started taking calls two hours before the game. In addition to the broadcast, we had extensive interaction with the restaurant customers, adding sports trivia questions and various prizes—mostly dinner certificates at Stanley's. It was an instant hit, and that momentum carried us for the next twenty years.

In addition to *Scrimmage Line*, I continued to assist Bill Pheiffer at the Salesianum football games, both as an analyst and doing play-by-play. I had become very comfortable behind the mic, but I never thought about it much more than as a hobby and a chance to interact with others in the sports world. Little did I realize that this introduction to radio and football broadcasting would lead to a much larger opportunity.

||||||||||||||||||||||||||||||||||||||||||||||||||||||||||||||||||||||||||||||||||||||||||||||

CHAPTER 20

Joining the Charity Golf Circuit

"Actually, Warren, I might have said you were the best pitcher of all time."

In 1983, I was approached with the idea of adding my name as chairman to a local annual celebrity golf tournament. I had participated in the Getty Leukemia Pro-Am during my playing days and always enjoyed the format and the chance to rub shoulders with some of the sports icons who played in it every year. It gave me a chance to assist with a worthy cause and just as with my broadcasting and public speaking, it complimented my sales and marketing efforts for Xerox.

At first, becoming chairman of the golf tournament seemed like a small commitment that would occupy a day or two of my time every June. But the event began to grow into a popular regional event with some of the talent we recruited to our expanded committee—business and government leaders like my fellow sales manager at Xerox, John Riley, along with Dave Press, Tom Ciconte, Charlie McDowell, John DiEleuterio, Tom Ogden, Jim Eversman, and Mike Harkins. We even added a tennis component led by local tennis champions, Gretchen Spruance and Jeff Olmstead.

As the tournament sponsor base expanded, we changed the name to "The Leukemia Classic." The bigger it grew, the greater the personal commitment. It reached a point where we began to plan for the next year the day after we said goodbye to the last celebrity leaving town. And it seemed that every year left us with a memory to last a lifetime.

One unforgettable encounter occurred during my second year as committee chairman. I had just walked up to the bar at the Wilmington Sheraton hotel with John Riley and PGA pro Fuzzy Zoeller to find famed "Yankee Clipper" Joe DiMaggio and pitching great Warren Spahn locked in conversation. What had started out as a discussion about the exploits of Phillies' pitcher Steve Carlton turned into a debate over the greatest pitcher of all time.

There was a crowd of professional athletes gathered around the baseball legends, jockeying for position to hear every word. Among them were baseball veterans Tommy Holmes and Sam McDowell, major league umpire Shag Crawford, and Dodger scout Ed Liberatore.

"Joltin Joe" was asking Spahn who he would choose as the greatest pitcher of all time. He was surprised by Spahn's response. "If I needed someone to pitch a game, for my life, I would choose Lew Burdette," answered Spahn. "No one pitched better under pressure than Lew." Burdette was a former battery mate of Spahn with the Milwaukee Braves.

DiMaggio responded, "Warren, that's not what I asked you. I said who do you feel is the greatest pitcher of all time. I might have said you!" (Spahn still holds the record for most wins by a left-handed major league pitcher although he lost three years to Army service in World War II, where he saw extensive combat.)

More people began to press in around the bar. John poked me and whispered, "Can you believe this?!"

At that point, Spahn switched gears. "No doubt, Joe, the greatest pitcher of all time is Sandy Koufax." DiMaggio asked why he had picked Koufax. Spahn's voice rose for everyone in the room to hear. "I know it for a fact, Joe, because I had to bat against him. And I could hit ... I hit more home runs than any pitcher in the history of baseball. You can look it up!"

At that point, Spahn jumped off the bar stool and announced that he was going to demonstrate for everyone what it was like to bat against Koufax. John poked me again, "Do you believe this?"

Spahn got down in his batting crouch in front of DiMaggio and quickly snapped back his head, simulating a Koufax pitch whizzing past him. "STRIKE ONE!" he yelled. He reset and then snapped back again, "STRIKE TWO!" He then narrated as to how he dug in for a third fast ball only to have Koufax fool him with a slider causing him to miss in a heap and collapse in the batter's box.

A roar went up at the bar and all headed in to find a table for dinner.

In addition to recruiting new committee talent, we decided to anchor the event each year with a paid attraction from the PGA Tour. We kicked off our first tournament in 1983 at Hercules Country Club with Chi Chi Rodriquez and netted $25,000 for leukemia research. Over the next ten years, this grew to as much as $200,000 a year.

In 1984, we recruited Masters and the soon to be U.S. Open champion Zoeller to fill our PGA Tour player role. Fuzzy was dealing with back issues at the time, and in 1985 would turn to Doctor Marcove for critical back surgery that would save his golf career. Although the good doctor was not much of a golfer, he made the journey down to Delaware on the couple of occasions when Fuzzy appeared.

Our event became so popular amongst the veteran and Hall of Fame baseball crowd, that author Jean Leavy's recent biography of Mickey Mantle, *The Last Boy*, included a reference to the tournament. The Philadelphia Phillies and Eagles were always well represented, along with NFL Hall of Famers like Randy White and Franco Harris. We also became a stop for Hollywood with regular appearances by Richard Roundtree (*Shaft*), Dennis Franz (*Hill Street Blues*), Dale Robertson (*Death Valley Days*), and my personal favorite, child star George "Spanky" McFarland of *Little Rascals* fame.

In those pre-Internet days, someone had stumbled upon an article about Spanky in which he mentioned that he enjoyed golf and had his own tournament in Texas. We found an address and sent Spanky a letter inviting him to Delaware. Thus, began a close friendship that lasted until his death in 1993.

A couple days before our event each June, Spanky would fly into Philadelphia, and John and I would pick him up and head to Stanley's Tavern. *My Scrimmage Line* broadcast partner Bill Bergey, a huge Spanky fan, would meet us and we would send out for some of Spanky's local special seafood requests—all of which he referred to as "steamers." After enjoying golf on Saturday and Sunday, he would join us at Hercules on Monday to entertain the sponsors and guests.

In an unfortunate twist of fate, one year we learned that Spanky's only granddaughter was diagnosed with childhood leukemia. With Spanky's permission, we ran a photo of him holding his granddaughter in his arms on the cover of our tournament program book.

As we were waiting for Spanky's golf clubs that year in the airport baggage area, we shared the book with him. The funny man we had come to know so well immediately broke down sobbing. It was quite a scene that I'm sure shocked the dozens of people gathered around the baggage belt, who had no idea who the chubby little man was crying his eyes out.

Just a few years later, Spanky called with sincere apologies that he would have to miss his annual trip to Delaware. Due to the nostalgia craze that was sweeping the country, there was a growing opportunity for paid appearances and as he said, "I have a family to feed." We wished him well, realizing that we might not see him again. In fact, about a year later, the phone rang and it was his wife, Doris, calling to say that Spanky had just died. She wanted us to know "how much he loved you guys and coming up to Delaware every year."

Another casualty of the renewed interest in nostalgia and the autograph craze sweeping the country was our friend Warren Spahn and the other old ballplayers like Joe DiMaggio, Brooks Robinson, Ralph Branca, Tommy Holmes, Larry Doby, and others. In the late 1980s, Spahn informed us that he would not make it back. He was headed to Atlantic City for paid appearances at the casinos and to sign autographs for cash.

Over a ten-year span beginning in 1983, we featured some of the biggest names in the world of golf. In addition to Rodriquez and Zoeller, greats like Arnold Palmer, Greg Norman, John Daly, Fred Couples, Payne Stewart, Ben Crenshaw, Johnny Miller, Paul Azinger, and Peter Jacobsen joined the cause.

Of course, the biggest name of all was the "King of Golf," Arnold Palmer. We were ambitious about the future of our event and concluded that an almost certain way to elevate its prestige was to recruit Arnie. Fortunately, our friend and committee member Howdy Giles was Arnie's personal dentist, friend, and photographer. Howdy loved the idea of bringing Arnie back to Delaware, so he led the way in negotiating a deal that could fit our budget and allow us to continue to raise the fundraising bar again.

Palmer competed in the Bell Atlantic senior tour event that weekend in nearby Malvern, Pennsylvania, finishing second. A tired Arnie attended and spoke briefly at our sponsor dinner Sunday evening before spending the night at the Giles home.

Refreshed and ready to go, Palmer arrived with Howdy the next morning, well before his scheduled time for the golf exhibition. As the golf legend exited Howdy's car, John Riley and I rushed over to greet him and help him with his clubs. Arnie pulled the clubs out of the trunk and noticed that John was wearing slacks with a Jack Nicklaus "Golden Bear" tab on the belt line.

Arnie suddenly yelled to Howdy, "Howdy, what the hell is that on John's pants!" Embarrassed, John responded, "Arnie, that's a golden bear." Arnie looked at him, feigning disgust and said, "That's not a bear, that's a pig!" John turned red while Arnie broke out laughing, telling Howdy he would have to teach John how to dress.

Each of our featured tour pros created a memory in their own way. Thirty years later, I still run into people who remember a particular moment. Perhaps the most memorable of all was in 1988 when Payne Stewart hit the shots and worked the crowd.

Just as engaging with the people as Arnie but certainly far more animated, Stewart challenged a group of three LPGA players to a match for his knickers. After what appeared to be a purposely missed four-foot putt on the last hole for a tie, he announced that "a bet is a bet" and promptly stripped his pants off in front of a gallery of a couple hundred. As he started to scamper off, we asked him to stop and pose for a few photos in his jockey shorts.

One of those photos appears in the book, "The Wackiest Moments in Golf." Later that night, Payne autographed the knickers and Spanky auctioned them off for a couple thousand dollars.

Joining Payne, Spanky, and me at the podium that night was a young leukemia patient named Steven Pelly. I always thought it important to ensure that we maintained our focus on the reason for all the fun we were having with the event. One way we did that was by having a young patient as our named ambassador every year. Tragically, we lost our first ambassador, Matt West, after only a year, but things were going better for young Steven after a bone marrow transplant. Everyone loved Steven, and he looked forward to our event more than anything in his life.

Spanky McFarland, Kevin, LPGA Pros Deborah McHaffie and Cindy Figg-Currier, Steve Pelly, and Payne Stewart

John Riley and I became quite close to Steven and his mother, and we often joined them for school events or when he was back in the hospital for treatments. In the year after Payne Stewart's appearance, Steven's health began to decline and, unfortunately, medical science was running out of options for our fourteen-year-old-buddy. One day, his mother Judy called and asked us to come to her home where Steven was lying on the couch in his final hours. This was the first time I was ever so close to a dying child, and it is an experience that will remain with me forever. Fortunately, due at least in some small way to the research dollars generated by our event, the survival rate from childhood leukemia is far greater today.

Ultimately, the celebrity/charity golf format became a victim of its own success. It became increasingly difficult to bring in the sports figures as events proliferated and options for the celebrities increased. More and more athletes wanted an appearance fee, so it became hard to justify paying one and not another.

Additionally, the tour pros became more expensive and their schedules hard to crack. One local athlete I got to know through the event was national amateur heavyweight boxing champion Henry Milligan. Henry had fought Mike Tyson in the semifinals of the 1984 Olympics and he had rapidly established a record of 11–0 as a pro. Soon our paths would cross in an adventure unlike any I had ever experienced before.

CHAPTER 21

A Business Detour –
Pro Management, Inc.

*"John, this is another fine mess you have gotten
me into!"*

t was one thing to host a celebrity golf tournament or a Monday
night sports call-in show, but what on earth was I doing on an
August day in 1986 at a weigh-in for the Friday night fights at
Resorts International in Atlantic City?

Boxing was a sport I knew nothing about, but suddenly I found
myself as the lead manager on fight day for the light heavyweight
fighter "Hammerin" Henry Milligan. In a few short years, Henry
had become the darling of the Delaware sports pages and a
serious threat to win a title. There was never a more unlikely
candidate for a boxing title. Henry was a Princeton-educated
engineer, member of Mensa, and until he walked into the ring,
a not-so-typical suburban middle-class kid. With a professional
record of eleven wins and one loss, that night was the comeback
fight after a shocking loss a few months before. The pressure was
on for Henry and his new management team—undefeated when
we took over, he was 0–1 under our leadership. Family, friends,
and probably Henry too, were questioning our sanity and our
competence.

So, how did I get myself into this situation? Like the Leukemia Golf Classic and a later unplanned trip to Africa, among other unconventional activities, I guess I could thank my friend and fellow sales manager John Riley.

The genesis of this adventure was when John, our hiring manager at Xerox, recruited Henry Milligan's brother Michael to join the company as a sales rep. Several months into Michael's tenure, he mentioned to John that Henry was rising in the ranks and needed additional talent to support him. He noted that a group of businessmen known as Cloverleaf backed the career of heavyweight champion Joe Frazier. So, against my better judgement, I joined with John, Henry, and an attorney friend of ours, Murray Sawyer, to form a sports management group that we titled Pro Management, Inc. (PMI).

The theory PMI proceeded under was that I had played professional sports, John and I had sales and marketing experience, and Murray brought the legal component. It sounded plausible, but none of us, aside from Henry, knew a lick about boxing. For boxing expertise we would retain Henry's current trainer/manager, and Atlantic City-based boxing consultant Pat Duffy.

As it turned out, Henry's previous manager was not interested in three new bosses, and he decided to step out of the picture. This meant we would rely almost entirely on Pat Duffy, a colorful fight figure who had been around the game since managing the 1960 U.S. Olympic team that featured young Cassius Clay. Pat knew everyone and everything about boxing. If he didn't know every detail immediately about a potential opponent, he would make a call or two to people he trusted and be back with answers quickly.

At the time we assumed control, Henry already had a Delaware-based fight pending. The venue would be the Delaware Park

Racetrack, which had hosted several boxing events in the past. There was a great deal of interest in this fight locally due to Henry's record and popularity. It took on added significance since it would be PMI's first contest managing Henry.

We looked at it almost as an exhibition for our friends and the hometown fans. Completely naïve about the risks and impressed with our new friend Pat Duffy, we accepted Pat's guidance, which was that the bout should not be much more than a modest workout as Henry prepared for the more serious competition in Atlantic City. I always remember Pat describing the other fighter, Al Shofner as, "just an opponent." In boxing jargon, this meant he was pretty close to a sure thing. Unfortunately, somebody forgot to tell Shofner.

The date of the fight conflicted with a sales promotion trip I had won to Hilton Head, South Carolina, so I would have to let Murray and John enjoy the Delaware Park fight festivities without me. At dinner that night, I was handed a message that I had a call at the front desk. On the other end of the line I could hear John yelling over the lobby noise, "Kevin, we lost! Henry was TKO'd in the second round."

Anyone that knows me as well as John does understands that I am a notorious practical joker, so my immediate reaction was that John was turning the tables on me and enjoying a laugh at my long-distance expense. "You're kidding me! Put Murray on the phone," I demanded. A couple minutes passed before our lawyer reached the phone and Murray repeated the unwelcome news.

I don't think I had felt a loss like this since my 1966 Salesianum football team was beaten by Middletown. The difference was that in football, I had some control. I immediately regretted allowing myself to get into this situation. I clearly had taken this "opportunity" too lightly. The next day, I could expect to be blamed on the sports pages for ruining Delaware's favorite son's promising boxing career. I think if I could have gotten my hand on John's throat at that moment, I could have choked him to death!

Fortunately, I had a couple more days to sort things out in my head before heading home to Wilmington. I thought to myself that whatever had just happened, it was certainly not as challenging as Sloan Kettering. I also had a chance to speak to Henry and could not have been more impressed with his dedication and commitment. This was a "fine mess I had gotten into," but my competitive juices began to flow again and it was no time to let Henry or my partners down.

So, three months later, I was in the center of championship boxing in Atlantic City. I had been staying close to Henry as much as possible as he prepped for the comeback fight. A natural 180 pounds, Henry had been knocking out fighters bigger than him since his days as an amateur heavyweight. He had won the 1983 National Amateur Heavyweight title by beating Henry Tillman before losing in the semifinals of the Olympic trials to none other than Mike Tyson. As a pro, Henry fought as a cruiserweight, but the team had decided for the comeback fight to go down a weight class to light heavyweight at 175.

I took a day off from my day job and joined Henry at the Jersey Shore the night before, as he continued to starve himself to get through the weigh-in the next morning. He was so worried about making weight that he stepped up on the scale stark naked. He made it by a few ounces.

The comeback fight was against Mike Fisher, a tough guy with an impressive record. The fight was a slugfest that went all eight rounds. There was no question that Henry's superior physical condition dominated in the later rounds, and he won by a unanimous decision. I do not know if it was more the thrill of victory or a sense of relief, but that night reversed the gloom felt by all of us just a few months before.

Henry soon added another win to up his record to 13–1, and Top Rank Boxing in New York approached us about a title fight. The contract called for two more Atlantic City based fights and then a title shot against Tommy "Hit Man" Hearns or Bobby Czyz—two of the big names in the game in the mid-'80s. To seal the deal Top Rank agreed to a signing bonus and we were off to prepare for the next bout in December.

One negative in Henry's TKO win that September was that he received a cut over his eye that took eight stitches to close. When I was in the emergency room with Henry that night, the doctor could not understand what on earth our corner man, Eddie "The Clot" Aliano, had put in the wound to close it. It was not the first time Henry sustained a cut, and we worried that this was a risk as he went up in class.

Shortly after signing with Top Rank, we received word that they had lined Henry up to fight Keith Vining of Detroit, another rising light heavyweight. Henry was excited and confident since he had beaten Vining once in their Golden Gloves days. The intensity of the workouts and trips to Philadelphia picked up as we neared the fight date in December. With about a week to go before the fight, things took a bad turn. Henry came down with the flu and Top Rank called to say that Vining had been injured and they were substituting with an Indiana fighter named Frank Minton.

When Pat Duffy received word of the switch to Minton, he was worried and urged us to cancel the fight. Minton's few losses were to top contenders and Pat felt that the speedy Minton's fighting style did not match up well against a slugger like Henry. Running a temperature of 102, we were more worried about Henry's health, so we contacted Top Rank and told them we wanted to cancel. All hell broke loose, with Top Rank threatening to cancel the contract or to sue. More importantly, Henry and his brother Michael wanted to go ahead with the fight. The team got together at my house to talk it out, but Henry and Michael stood their ground—the fight would go ahead.

During the early rounds of the Minton fight, Henry suffered a cut and a broken nose, but aside from all the blood, it was a close fight. Between rounds, Eddie "The Clot" tried to work his magic with the referee directly in Henry's face checking his condition. Unfortunately, the bleeding wouldn't stop and over Henry's protests the referee called the fight. I spent the rest of the night in the emergency room with Henry where they did confirm that his nose had been broken—again.

By the next day, Murray, John, and I had decided it was time to have a serious discussion with Henry about his future in the game. What always weighed on us was that Henry was a young man with alternatives in life. No question that he could win more fights, but we worried that the constant pounding in the sparring sessions might do more damage than the big battles in the Atlantic City arena. When we met later in the day, Henry was open to stepping aside for a while, but clearly, it was hard to part with a dream.

We did agree to continue PMI. We had learned that three potential NFL recruits from the University of Delaware, including future league MVP, Rich Gannon, were looking for representation. We assisted running back Bob Norris and tight end Jeff Modisett with their contracts, but Gannon's situation proved more complicated. Taken in the fourth round of the draft by New England, they announced they wanted to convert Rich from quarterback to defensive back. Gannon wanted no part of that arrangement and refused to sign. As the saying goes, "That was above our pay grade," so we agreed to release Rich from his relationship with us to work with a more experienced agent. Later, when Norris and Modisett were cut, we closed out of the sport's agent business and went back to fully concentrate on our day jobs.

Kevin, John, and Murray Sawyer with boxers
Henry Milligan and Dave Tiberi

CHAPTER 22

Divorce: The Shock and the Recovery

"This is going to take a few weeks for me to get over."

A ccording to the American Psychological Association, the divorce rate in the United States is in the forty to fifty percent range. There is some debate and confusion around these numbers, but the fact is that divorce is now fairly common in today's America. Rates have generally been growing since WWII. Having grown up in a very tight-knit traditional family, if I ever thought of divorce at all, it was something that happened to other people. It never crossed my mind that it would ever happen in my life. Family to me was just something I took for granted—it would always be at the center of my world.

In 1996, life was rolling along very nicely for me. It had been sixteen years since my amputation, and there were no signs of the desmoid returning. I had adapted fairly well to my one-armed world, my son Brett was entering his second year at Villanova, my daughter Erin was doing well at Philadelphia Textile (now Philadelphia University), and my daughter Brie would soon be entering her senior year at Brandywine High School in Wilmington.

That same year, my wife, Cathy, had received an offer to play her banjo at Walt Disney World under a contract that would keep her there about half the year. She had played for years in her father's band, but now she was with a new group getting rave reviews. It was no surprise to me that Cathy was a big hit in Orlando. She was extremely talented. Although the kids missed their mother and I missed my wife, we managed things in her absence and were happy for her success.

I knew when I married Cathy that her first love was her banjo and her music, but I never imagined that she would leave our life of twenty years together to pursue that dream. Obviously, I missed the many signs along the way.

Cathy dropped the bomb when she came home on a break that winter. There was no talking, counseling, or negotiating—the decision was final and irreversible. She returned to Florida and the marriage was over by August of 1997.

To say I was in shock would not adequately describe my state of mind. The only thing I can compare it to is a sudden death or suicide in the family, where you are left with emotional wreckage and endless questions but nowhere to go for answers. I had somehow stood up to a disease that had tried to destroy me, but my health crisis had played out over years and I could see that something had to give in the end. During those days, I had my moments of doubt and weakness, but it did not register like the shock of this event on the eve of our daughter's graduation and our twentieth wedding anniversary.

These new emotions were at an intensity level that I had never experienced in my life. I was hurt, humbled, depressed, and fearful, but most of all heartbroken. Then my brain shifted to embarrassment and anger. I was in a downward spiral and holed up in my parents' home for days trying to get a grip on things. I asked myself over and over again, "How did I not see this coming? How could I be so blind?"

I worried how it would affect my relationship with my children. I hated myself for not being strong. I was supposed to be the one to support them and others emotionally. I began to question my faith in God. After all I had been through, how could this added cross be sent to me to bear?

In the mental fog during those days, I was so oblivious to the world around me that I didn't notice the support that began to surround me. Roles suddenly reversed as my kids, who were then entering young adulthood, stepped up to provide tremendous support and comfort to me. But I couldn't help but feel that we had let them down with the sudden breakup of our family.

After spending days at my parents' home, I returned to work knowing I had to get a grip on things and get back into a daily routine. I told myself I had to draw on the strength and experience that had gotten me through the loss of my arm and the loss of my pro football ambitions. I had to draw again on the "four Fs" to save me from drowning: faith, family, friends, and fortitude.

To begin to turn things around, I had to admit to myself I needed help. I turned to my personal physician, Bill Taylor. A fellow Salesianum graduate with an engaging manner, he was more than a doctor and friend. Bill agreed to see me the same day I called him and instinctively sensed my visit would take more time than the usual twenty minutes. We set the appointment for the end of his day.

At 5:30, he called me into his office and I unloaded for the next thirty minutes. He listened attentively without interruption and then said, "Two things, Kev. I'm going to prescribe some medicine for you so you can get some sleep, and I'm going to refer you to a counselor that I believe can help get you through this."

"I don't want to see a counselor," I replied, rather foolishly. "I think that's a sign of weakness, and I don't want on my record that I saw a shrink." Bill then patiently walked me through the benefits of counseling and why even the strongest men and women can benefit from talking to a professional during times of great emotional upheaval—times when we are unable to think clearly and make good decisions. Although reluctant, I trusted Bill's advice and soon contacted the counselor he recommended.

At work the following day, I met with my boss, Joe Teti, and told him, "This is going to take a few weeks for me to get over."

Born and raised on the streets of South Philadelphia, Joe was tough, self-made and devoted to his own family. "Kevin," he said. "I think this is going to take longer than a few weeks, but we got your back until you recover."

Joe's support and the response from others in the office helped a great deal, so I swallowed more of my pride and headed to Stanley's Tavern that night for my two-hour radio show. As soon as I walked in the door, the big bear himself, Bill Bergey, grabbed me and took me into a corner to find out what had happened and to offer his support. My co-host, Don Voltz, carried me through the two-hour *Scrimmage Line* program.

As I continued through what I guess I would best describe as a grieving process, the word about Cathy leaving me had spread like wildfire. My three sisters, Patty, Megan, and Kerry, were there for me every day, along with my children. Rather than creating a divide with my children, the pending divorce was bringing us closer in many respects. Friends such as Dave Jenkins, John Riley, John Bunting, Larry Pietropaulo, my brother Sean, and others also took turns carrying me through the first month.

Because I could not sleep, I signed up for Eucharistic adoration at my parish church, Immaculate Heart of Mary. Taking the 2:00

to 3:00 AM shift gave me time to think and return to prayer as a source of strength and comfort. I soon began to realize that as in the case of my health crisis, my faith as well as family and friends were playing a critical role in my recovery. Through these sources of support, I would again find the fortitude to climb out of the deep, dark hole I was in.

But it takes more than love and prayer sometimes to clear out the chaos in your mind during a deeply emotional crisis. For me, a pathway would be found through my time in counseling. Dr. Taylor had recommended that I see a woman by the name of Doris Mecal. Doris was no ordinary counselor. Her own life experiences were such that she could listen and speak with a certain authenticity that gave me a confidence like no one I had ever known.

I found that I could talk to Doris about anything. We discussed how I could become a better father, a better son, a better brother, and a better Catholic. Together, we identified the baggage I needed to get rid of in my life—things like complaining, blaming, arrogance, pride, anxiety, and fear.

Doris also helped me to realize that alcohol was not my friend— that I needed to turn in a different direction to relieve stress. Social drinking and drinking in response to stress was such a part of my life that I had never considered the possibility that life could be better without that dependency. Doris's counsel along with a nudge from family, enabled me to set out on a course that would improve my life more than any other single step. One of the most rewarding elements in recent years has been to help others as they faced up to their own need to choose a life of sobriety.

Looking back on my time in counseling, I could probably say that it was the first time in my life that I was completely honest with another human being. From my earliest days, I always felt that I had a certain image to uphold. Due to the breakup of my marriage, much of that image had been shattered. With Doris, I could drop the façade I put up for the rest of the world and get on with a plan for the rest of my life.

Sometimes life needs to knock you off your feet to get your attention. During my dark days, I felt that God had abandoned me, but now my faith was again a source of strength. I believe that God had a plan for me to see how much I could take and if I could handle it. If I made it, I would not only make more of my life but would enable me to do more for others. This entire experience, as difficult as it was to endure, reinforced for me four important principles:

- No man or woman is an island. At some time in our lives, we are going to have to rely on family and friends to help keep us afloat.

- If you want to improve your life and achieve happiness, be honest with yourself and identify the barriers and bad habits that are holding you back. It is never too late in life to make changes.

- Life moves on. Don't dwell on any misfortune and let it rent space in your head. Learn from the challenge, adapt and implement new behaviors going forward.

- Never, ever lose faith. My faith in God and the power of prayer has been a major source of strength for me and can be for others as well.

||||||||||||||||||||||||||||||||||||||||||||||||||||||||||||||||||||||||||||||||||||||

CHAPTER 23

Getting in Shape – The Marine Corps Marathon

"You're fat! Get the hell back in the gym."

n the days and weeks after returning home from my surgery in 1979, I was extremely weak. The eleven-and-a-half-hour operation, blood transfusions, and the energy-draining healing process had me totally worn out. I was sleeping eight to ten hours each night, followed by long naps later in the day. I think I was sleeping, eating, and resting as much as I had my first year as an infant. The good news was, that apart from the nagging phantom sensation, I was pain free for the first time in eighteen months.

It was also the holiday season. That, combined with my extended inactivity, resulted in me adding some pounds, especially around the waist. Then in late January, I was booked to do my first official speaking engagement since my operation. It was for the annual sports banquet of the St. Edmond's Academy for Boys near Wilmington. Putting on a suit and tie for the occasion, I had trouble buttoning my pants and the top button on my shirt. I remember thinking that Frank the amputee, who counseled me back at Sloan Kettering, was certainly right about the potential for weight gain after amputations. His statistical claim of gaining an average of forty pounds in eighteen to twenty-four months was beginning to hit home. In only two months I had gained at least twenty pounds.

It felt good to get back in the public speaking saddle and these kids and their parents were just the audience that I needed to help me gain my confidence back. Several of the parents came up to me afterwards, thanking me for the speech and wishing me well. Lagging in the rear of the line was my old friend Joe Biden, the young Delaware U.S. Senator and future Vice President whose sons Beau and Hunter attended St. Edmonds. After a few pleasant remarks, the senator put his hand on my right shoulder and said just loud enough for me to hear, "You're fat! Get the hell back in the gym." As we say in Delaware, that was "Joe being Joe," but I took it as a friend delivering a much-needed wake-up call.

It was clearly time for me to put a workout plan in place. I started slowly, doing a half-mile jog at the Brandywine YMCA indoor track. After two weeks of running, I was up to a mile. Four weeks later, I could jog two miles and the weight was beginning to come off, although not quickly enough for me. So, I started to think about other little athletic mountains I might be able to climb. I was running regularly, and my balance was improving due in part to the racquetball I was also playing. I began to enter 5k races, and in the back of my mind thought that maybe I could someday run in the Delaware Caesar Rodney Half Marathon—something that had always been on my life bucket list.

For the next several years, I ran in more and more 5k races, always with the Caesar Rodney on my mind. To run a half-marathon, I would need a plan and a training schedule. So, in October 1995, I made the commitment to try but immediately began to doubt myself. Would I fail and completely embarrass myself? The Caesar Rodney was not just any half-marathon. It had a reputation as one of the toughest courses in the country. Much of the course has long uphill climbs, followed by such steep declines that it can quickly force tired runners out of control. For four years, the Villanova long-distance runners would get directions from me to Wilmington to run in the event, only to return to the dorm grumbling about the level of difficulty.

Always exhausted and feeling like I could not run another hundred yards after finishing a 5k, I wondered how I would compete on a course that was four times the distance. But I was assured by experienced runners that if I put in the training time and mileage, I could succeed. Then, in March of 1996, an exhausted one-armed man crossed the finish line of the Caesar Rodney half-marathon at the two-hour mark. It was a great relief. One of the first thoughts that entered my mind after finishing was that there was no way I could ever run a full marathon.

I ran two more Caesar Rodney's over the next three years and came to the realization that like other things in life, the more you do it, the better you get. This was also the time when I was dealing with my divorce and the additional baggage that went with it. I found that the pain of running helped to focus my mind and keep it off the emotional pain surrounding the breakup of our family.

Running the Caesar Rodney with daughter Brie

To get on track for my new goal of a full marathon, I decided to seek additional running advice. This led to a four-month marathon training program. Again, I had my doubts but was assured by experienced runners that if I followed the plan, the race would be anti-climactic. Three other friends decided they would train and run with me, so as a team of four, we signed up for the Marine Corps Marathon in Washington, DC—the ninth largest marathon in the world.

My partners were longtime friend Tom Pitts, whom I had worked with at Xerox for twenty-four years, and two new running buddies, Bob Chris and Ivan Avendano. I was forty-nine years old at the time, and both Bobby and Tom, two ex-Marines, were in their late fifties. Ivan, who was originally from Mexico, worked with Bobby at Boeing as an electrician. Ivan was a very strong runner, often winning his age group in the 5k's we had run.

During our months of preparation, Tom always kept things loose. He was what I would describe as a professional "ball buster." Bobby, on the other hand, could complain about almost anything, except for perhaps a cold Budweiser. Ivan was the quiet guy, but when he spoke, it was usually hilarious. We trained as a team following our four-month plan, which basically amounted to "lots of time on your feet running or jogging."

Things began to get intense about twelve weeks prior to the race. The focus was our Saturday run where we would ratchet up the mileage from one week to the next. At week fourteen, our Saturday jog took two-and-a-half hours. Because we were running in August and September, we had to consume liquids about every four to five miles to stay hydrated. By the time we reached the Saturdays where we ran twenty miles or more, it would take all day Sunday to recover.

I ran our twenty-two-mile Saturday with Bobby a week before the marathon. It was drizzling and about seventy degrees, and we made the journey in just less than four hours. For the first time in our running lives, we both experienced what they call the "runner's high." We were becoming confident we could now do this, and we were like two kids sprinting the last quarter mile to the finish. We celebrated by drinking a couple of cold beers which felt like they were injected into our blood stream as our dehydrated bodies sucked in the liquid.

Although I had played professional football in stadiums filled with over 70,000 fans, I found myself a bit intimidated on race day by the very sight of 30,000 runners gathered near the nation's capital. It was also an adventure figuring out the bathroom arrangements. We were to line up according to our anticipated average mile time with banners depicting five-minute milers, seven-minute milers, etc. When Bobby, Tom and I got to our ten-minute miler holding area, I heard some people shout out my name.

*Preparing for the
Marine Corps Marathon*

To my surprise, it was three teenage boys and a representative from Delaware Special Olympics heading to the eight-minute area. As focused as I was on my own challenge that lay ahead, it gave me chills to think how far these kids had come in their development. At Xerox, we ran the swimming event at Delaware Special Olympics each year, and I knew all three boys since they were less than ten. Here they were running in the Marine Corps Marathon starting ahead of half the field of runners. Thirty years ago, this would have been unthinkable, but since the inception of Special Olympics, kids with disabilities were doing things society had never considered them capable of. With my own little challenge to overcome, I had something in common with these heroic teenagers. It gave me just the shot of adrenalin that I needed to get started.

Temperatures that October morning were heading into the upper seventies, less than ideal conditions for a twenty-six-mile race. Race officials were warning everyone to be sure to take water at each water stop. Running together, it took us three minutes just to reach the starting line due to the faster runners crowded between us and the start. At mile four, we reached the first jam-packed water station.

Runners had to stop due to the number of people trying to fill up and hydrate. I was wearing a green t-shirt that had a simple phrase that said, "X Man's Army." It was designed by a family member in honor of my father, Francis X. Reilly's seventieth birthday. Apparently, the Marines who were manning the water stops interpreted the shirt as belonging to an Army wounded warrior and they started giving me preferential treatment at the water stations, yelling, "Sir, back here, sir" and guiding me behind the water station where there was no crowd. This was much to the chagrin of my two, real-life Marine vet buddies who were fighting their way at every stop.

At mile fifteen, I was separated from Tom and Bobby, but kept cruising along until mile nineteen. Suddenly, a guy dressed in a Gumby costume, of all things, flew past me skipping and hopping. For some reason, this completely blew my concentration and with six miles to go, I started to fade. Struggling badly as I reached mile twenty-four, out of nowhere I heard people screaming my name.

Up ahead, I saw a vision. There was my Philadelphia Eagles jersey with #52 on it. It was my son Brett, now twenty-one and a student at Villanova. As my pace and heart rate picked up, I could see two screaming women with him. I couldn't believe my eyes—it was my two daughters, Erin and Brie. All three had decided on the spur of the moment that morning to drive from college to Washington to catch me running in the race. How they found me was a minor miracle, but what a lift it gave me. Adrenalin that I didn't think I had kicked in, as tears ran down my face during mile twenty-four and twenty-five.

But the sudden burst of energy soon disappeared and the last mile became a nightmare. I knew I was in trouble the minute I stopped sweating. First came the chills, then the cramps. Runners were down all around me, with medics holding IV bottles. I could not look at them for fear their condition was contagious. With a half a mile to go, my calves cramped and I could barely bend my legs. Panic set in as I thought my legs were about to give out completely. Then, out of nowhere, my sister Kerry jumped the racecourse fence and ran next to me to keep me going. Nearly delirious, I could barely comprehend that I had finished the race.

After gulping down some water, my head started to clear and I could make out the iconic Iwo Jima flag-raising monument in the background. I was filled with pride. I had run a marathon! The Marine Corps Marathon!

‖‖‖

CHAPTER 24

Growing as a Motivational Speaker

"Kevin, you need to increase your earnings or you may be facing bankruptcy."

After retiring from Xerox in 2006, one of my goals was to improve as a motivational speaker. I had been speaking to various groups since my early days as a Philadelphia Eagle but with little focus. Even at that time, I would strive to inspire my audience in some way. Maybe for a high school student to go out for the team and give it their best shot or for a salesman to make one more call that day in a quest for top performance. If a guy with limited talent like me could become captain of special teams for a great NFL franchise, they could make it in their field or chosen profession. After my surgery, I clearly had a far stronger platform and the potential to carry an important message. I just needed to get better at what I did to reach my audience.

Public speaking for me really began in my first year with the Eagles. My total salary in 1973 was $17,000. I would estimate that the Eagles team payroll for fifty players and coaching staff was only in the ballpark of three million dollars. While I was on the bottom rung of the salary ladder, there were few players at that time who exceeded $100,000 per year. (The league minimum salary today for a player who makes the roster is $500,000 a year.) Therefore, every Eagle player I knew supplemented his salary by working in the off season. For me, it was substitute teaching or speaking engagements. About three days a week, I taught at Collingdale High School in Collingdale, Pennsylvania, and began what would ultimately become a second career doing speaking engagements as an Eagles player.

When I was in the league, there were no structured workouts or mandatory mini-camps like there are today. After the season back then, most players headed back to wherever they called home. I recall there were twelve to fifteen of us living in the Philadelphia-area during that offseason in 1973. With the addition of quarterback Roman Gabriel, middle linebacker Bill Bergey, and new head coach Mike McCormack, the Eagles improved to a 5–8–1 season following a dismal 2–11–1 season in 1972. Eagle fans were getting excited about the upcoming season.

Jim Gallagher, then the Eagles public relations director, was getting besieged with player speaking requests. More than half of the requests came from youth and high school sports banquets or charitable fundraising groups. Very few were paying gigs, except for corporations or businesses that typically requested our All-Pro stars such as Gabriel, Bergey, wide receiver Harold Carmichael, or safety Bill Bradley. Being a local guy who came up through the youth sports system and who competed against Philadelphia high school teams when I played for Salesianum, I was a perfect fit for the non-paying banquets and events.

PR director Gallagher saw these speaking requests as an opportunity to build the fan base, so he approached me three weeks after the '73 season with a deal. For every free speaking engagement that I accepted, he would pay me $150 to do the next one. He called this our "Irish secret." I gave about fifteen speeches that year and in 1974, following my second full year as an Eagle, I delivered forty-five.

Just like anything else that we do repetitively, I got better and more confident with every talk—learning to read the audience, experimenting to see what message had the most impact and what was received better than others. And yes, oh yes, I borrowed shamelessly from a few seasoned professionals who occasionally graced the dais with me, especially in the joke department. I often used borrowed material from two old pros in the region, Cozy Morley and Jimmy Joyce.

After retiring from the NFL in 1977, my speaking opportunities dropped off considerably to around a half-dozen times a year, due in large part to my growing family, my job, and my health. Following my physical recovery from the 1979 amputation, I started doing motivational talks centered around my ongoing struggle with desmoid disease and the recovery process.

Going about my life each day, I incorporated some of the philosophy that I had absorbed during my hospital talk with Rocky Bleier. I wanted to convey that message to others. Not just those who struggled with health challenges, but all of us who hold back in life due to fear of failure.

As I described in the previous chapter, in 1996, I took on one of those challenges where you know you will push yourself to the outer limits to a place where you knew there would be a serious chance of failure. I ran two half-marathons, and then a full marathon.

While recovering from my amputation at Sloan Kettering, I was told by the helpful veteran that I should avoid running due to balance and other issues. That nagging thought had resided in my head since the surgery and I wanted to prove to myself I could do it. It also occurred to me that while it may be hard for most people to put themselves in my shoes as an amputee, people could relate to someone pushing themselves beyond normal limits through a marathon. So, going forward, this was something I could work into my talks to add real-world balance to my message of overcoming the adversity of a life-threatening illness and amputation. Running a marathon was something many people could relate to.

During the '80s and through the early '90s, I increased my speaking pace and was able to modestly increase my fees. But I felt like I was on speaker cruise control and not improving much during that period. I would probably grade myself at a B-level performance—not truly growing as a speaker or adding much in the way of new material into my talks.

My divorce, though, sent me into a tailspin, emotionally and financially.

I already mentioned the four "Fs" in my life: faith, family, friends, and fortitude. It was in 1996 as I was going through the process of the divorce that I found I needed them most. It became nearly impossible for me to focus on anything, from my finances, house, and career—and, most importantly, my children. Ironically, as difficult as divorce would be, it turned out to have a positive impact on my speaking career.

Divorces are both emotional and expensive, and I soon found myself facing major financial challenges. My former PMI partner and friend Murray Sawyer was counseling me with respect to my personal affairs and had some basic advice: "Kevin, you need to increase your earnings or you may be facing bankruptcy." The very sound of that shook me to my core.

I was in no position to change my Xerox career at that point, so the best avenues open to me were to do more speaking engagements and develop my broadcasting career. Murray's advice was to take every opportunity that came along. "You will get better at it and things will begin to fall in place," he said.

Murray was right on both counts! Within two years, I was putting money in the bank. Because I was improving, demand for my appearances grew, and I began receiving higher fees. I also expanded my broadcasting work with the Philadelphia Eagles and WIP radio—an adventure that would continue for the next sixteen years.

Motivating the Baltimore Ravens during training camp

CHAPTER 25

|||||||||||||||||||||||||||||||||||||||||||||||||||||||||||||||||||||||||||||||||||||

Flying Again with the Eagles

"Reilly, this ain't radio. Tell them what they can't see!"

I n Chapter 19, I discussed how I got my start in broadcasting by paying my dues at a local Delaware radio station. That sideline was more like a hobby for me up until 1998, when fate seemed to intervene once again in my life.

In my role as marketing manager for Xerox's Philadelphia region, I put together a deal to exchange the use of Xerox products for various packages of tickets for Eagles games to be used for our customer base. My point of contact for the Eagles was their marketing director, Dave Rowan. Knowing about my experience as an Eagle and having been on our *Scrimmage Line* show as a guest at one time, Dave asked if I would be interested in joining an expanded format for Eagles radio broadcasts.

The official station for Eagles games was WYSP-FM, but they had competition before and after the games from WIP, Philly's all-sports radio station. The challenge for WYSP was that WIP began their broadcast at 10:00 AM and fans would fail to switch back to WYSP before the game, thus missing the WYSP pre-game broadcast. WYSP and the Eagles saw an opportunity to both compete with WIP in the 10:00 to 11:00 hour and lure back listeners for their own pre-game show.

Rowan and the radio team decided they wanted to launch the new pre-game show, *Countdown to Kickoff*, with new voices. In addition to myself, they recruited former TV sportscaster John Miller to co-host the show. We were also asked to co-host a new post-game show called *The 5th Quarter*. This gig would last for the next fourteen years and lead to lots of interesting encounters.

As you might expect, the *Countdown* hour was always filled with excitement and anticipation. There is no doubt in my mind that Eagles fans are the most passionate in the country—and hope would spring eternal as we fielded calls leading up to game time. During the Andy Reid years, with a winning coach and team, there were lots of opportunities to cheer on the Eagles, as we were headed to the playoffs most years.

The 5th Quarter was an entirely different matter. Even a win by two or three touchdowns would often be followed by calls from a steady stream of perfectionists who decried every move made by Coach Reid. They would be particularly frustrated by what they thought was Reid's tendency to play it safe and sit on a lead, which would sometimes result in a comeback by the opponent. Working for the team, John and I were in a tough spot when we sometimes agreed with the caller but had to find a way to be supportive while remaining credible.

With Bill Bergey and award-winning sportswriter Ray Didinger

No doubt, some of our more animated callers had been fueled by a few beers before, during and after the game. This became particularly evident after Sunday or Monday night games when we did not come on the air until after midnight. It didn't take long to begin to dread these games, especially the ones that went into overtime. When the season schedule was announced, the first thing I did was to scan the sheet to see how many late games we would be facing.

The "show of shows" finally occurred on February 6, 2005. For the first time since 1980, the Eagles had made it to the big dance. Following our intro music that day, John Miller proudly announced, "Live from Alltel Stadium in Jacksonville, it's the Super Bowl *Countdown to Kickoff* Show. I'm John Miller, along with former Eagle linebacker Kevin Reilly, getting you ready for Super Bowl XXXIX between the Philadelphia Eagles and the New England Patriots."

It was a great moment. We were kicking off the hometown radio broadcast for the Super Bowl while sitting in the press box looking out at the field that in three hours would be watched by an estimated eighty-six million viewers around the world. And the competitors were two of the teams I had played for!

There were seven of us in the booth, including John, myself, Bill Bergey, producer Joe McPeak, legendary Eagles play-by-play announcer Merrill Reese, Mike Quick, and Noel Reese, Merrill's son. Right before kickoff, Merrill turned around with a big smile and gave us the thumbs up. This was the moment Philly fans had been waiting for—for two-and-a-half decades!

Unfortunately, victory was not to be. The Eagles battled Tom Brady and the Pats down to the wire but ended up on the short end of a 24–21 score.

About the same time, another opportunity fell into my lap—the chance to work televised college games for Comcast Sports Net. Comcast wanted to expand their market by reaching fans interested in FCS football. Formerly known as IAA, the Football Championship Subdivision (FSC) included teams like Richmond, Delaware, and Villanova. Many of the teams were followed closely by fans and alumni in the Philadelphia region.

The broadcasts were organized into two teams with former Eagle fullback Jon Ritchie on the "A" team. I joined as an analyst for the "B" team, but was soon moved up when John moved to ESPN. This was my first shot at TV broadcasting and I loved it! The increased exposure compared to radio was significant. I soon found that while I might receive

Another game at the Link

a dozen comments about our broadcast in the week after a game on radio, with TV, I would receive a couple dozen comments the day after alone.

One day in the Eagles press room, I was complimented by one of the members of the national broadcast team in town to cover the Eagles. He had picked up my game on Saturday and liked what he saw. I felt pretty good about his positive comments, but then something he said stopped me dead in my tracks. "Kevin, it's a shame that you'll never be able to do an NFL game," he said. "Not because you lack the talent, but because the league would never put an amputee on the air. They would see it as a distraction to the audience."

I tried not to take his comment personally, but it was pretty deflating. I filed it away, and used it as motivation to overcome another hurdle.

Being in the right place at the right time seemed to be a pattern in my broadcasting career up to that point, and so it was to happen again. In the summer of 2012, I was approached by Eagles television director Rob Alberino and Fox NFL producer Artie Kempner about doing play-by-play for the upcoming pre-season games.

The idea was to try something different by placing three knowledgeable, but heavily biased ex-Eagles in the booth, instead of the usual neutral national broadcast team. I would be joined by former Jets head coach and Eagles cornerback Herm Edwards and former Eagle defensive end Hugh Douglas. I was assigned to do the play-by-play, Herm would be the coaching analyst, and Hugh, a real character, would be comic relief and player insider.

Before the first broadcast, Artie gave us instructions, including telling us to put our phones in our pockets on vibrate and to not look at them until halftime—otherwise, they could be a major distraction. All three of us were nervous and got off to a shaky start. When we went to our first commercial break, I checked in with Artie to see how we were doing. He shouted over the noise, "Reilly, this ain't radio. Tell them what they can't see!" Time for a course correction.

Meanwhile, my phone was vibrating non-stop. Herm turned to me and said, "My phone feels like it's going to explode in my pocket." Wondering what the hell was going on, Herm looked at his phone. There was a text from his friend and mentor, Tony Dungy. It said, "Herm, the story has leaked!"

We looked at each other. *What story?* Artie came over to our earphones just then. "Everybody, listen-up, because I only have thirty seconds until we are back live," he said. "Reilly, when we come back on, I want you to say, 'Breaking news just in—Michael Vick has signed a contract with the Eagles. Herm, you follow with just coach-speak on what his skills can do for the team, and Hugh … no dog jokes!'"

Just our luck, one of the biggest Eagles or NFL stories in years, and everyone was caught off guard. We were stuck making it up as we went along. I'm not sure I completely recovered from the shaky start, and frankly, I didn't feel comfortable in the role of play-by -play. But I had had my shot. After the game, Artie approached me. "Kevin," he said. "I believe you are the first amputee to ever do an NFL game on TV." That meant more to me than Artie probably realized.

On the sideline at Veterans Stadium
as an Eagles broadcaster

|||||||||||||||||||||||||||||||||||||||||||||||||||||||||||||||||||||||||||||||||||||||||||||||||||||||||||||||||||||||||||||||||

CHAPTER 26

Those That Inspire

"Kevin, if God took all the working parts of our bodies, he'd still be four fingers short. How about that?"

L ate one spring evening in 1991, with my kids in bed and my wife asleep, I relaxed on the couch after watching a Phillies game. After the game was over, I began channel surfing and stopped quickly at the *Larry King Show*. I recognized his guest, San Francisco Giants pitcher Dave Dravecky, who was discussing a health issue.

Fascinated by his story and seeing the replay of him breaking his arm, I listened intently as the interview with Larry King continued. As King wrapped up the interview, he asked, "This wasn't a cancerous tumor, is that right Dave?"

"It's called a desmoid tumor," Dravecky responded. "And it does not metastasize."

Hearing the word *desmoid* shocked me. The disease was so rare that in the twelve years since my surgery, I had never heard the word mentioned outside a small circle of people at Sloan Kettering. I do not remember a word Dravecky said after that, but I remember literally screaming at the TV loud enough to wake the neighbors.

After shaking off the shock that a fellow professional athlete had the same rare disease as me, my mind filled with thoughts of all the pain and futility I had lived with before a doctor at Sloan Kettering saved my life. The fact was that one doctor after another failed to diagnose the disease. They had never seen it before—they didn't know what they didn't know. I felt compelled to contact Dravecky to see if I could steer him to the right help.

Dravecky mentioned he was going back into surgery soon, so I knew I had to get a hold of him quickly if I were to refer him to Dr. Marcove and Sloan Kettering. They were the only doctor and medical team I was aware of that was fully capable of handling his case. They were the only ones knowledgeable and skilled enough to get the margins needed in the surgical battle against desmoid. But how would I contact him? I couldn't sleep at all that night knowing that I had to find a way. Then it hit me—Dallas Green.

Dallas Green was a former Phillies pitcher and manager of the team when they won the 1980 World Series. He later managed the New York Yankees. Green had been raised in Newport, Delaware and played ball at Conrad High School and the University of Delaware. I had known Dallas for fifteen years, and I was certain he was someone who could get through the screened calls in San Francisco and in touch with Dave Dravecky. When I called Dallas and explained the situation, he said, "No problem champ, I'll get back to you tomorrow." Two days later, he called me to tell me that the Dravecky family, with only days to go until the pitcher's surgery, had circled the wagons around him and were holding off all his calls.

I was disappointed, but not surprised, remembering my own inclination to avoid calls from many well-meaning friends and family during my own crisis. Then another idea hit me—contact my friend Jason Stark, baseball writer for *USA Today*. I knew

Jason when he was working for the *Philadelphia Inquirer* as their Phillies beat writer.

Jason also attempted to reach Dravecky without success, but he shared the story with Bill Fleishman of the *Philadelphia Daily News*, who wrote an article about how I was trying to get in touch with him to help.

The good news was that Dravecky found his way to Sloan Kettering and his amputation was performed by a colleague of Dr. Marcove. Soon after his surgery, I received a call from him. He was the

first desmoid patient I would give advice to. Due to my ongoing work with the Desmoid Tumor Foundation, there have been many more since then.

Today, Dave Dravecky travels the country speaking about his ordeal and providing guidance to others on meeting life's greatest challenges. Dave and his wife, Jan, have founded a non-profit organization called "Endurance with Jan & Dave Dravecky." A quote on their website says, "We realized through our own experience that one cannot face adversity in life alone, so we have created this organization to help others endure on the journey."

Having my own form of cancer and acquired disability, I found myself drawn to the cause of supporting organizations such as Easter Seals and Special Olympics, as well as responding to requests for individual counseling to cancer victims and amputees. Meeting so many adults and children with severe illnesses or special needs, my heart goes out to the parents.

I am always amazed to be around these special families. They go about their daily lives without complaint and even find time to help others. It always drives home the point to me that while we cannot always control the hand we are dealt, we have enormous power within us to control how we respond to it.

In a strange way, my affliction has been a gift because it has given me the opportunity to meet and in some cases become involved in the life of extraordinary people. Four individuals I have learned a lot about courage, caring and resilience from—Andrew McDonough, Keith Powell, Matt Szczur, and Jon Reynolds— have stories that are worth telling.

I have known the McDonough family since 1975. They lived across the street from my first wife, Cathy. I recall throwing the football around with their boys during my NFL days. Their son Joe soon married and he and his wife, Chris, had a daughter and a son. Their boy, Andrew, developed into a soccer star in the youth leagues and took his talent to my alma mater, Salesianum.

On January 27, 2007, Andrew helped lead his travel soccer team to victory in the Pennsylvania state championship soccer tournament. Within forty-eight hours, he was in septic shock and cardiac arrest. Andrew's diagnosis was acute myeloid leukemia (or AML), a cancer of the bone marrow and the blood. His prognosis was grim. As he slipped into a coma, doctors did not expect Andrew to last through that first night. But not only would he make it through the night, he kept up the fight with his family at his side for the next 167 days while undergoing nearly fifty surgical procedures and being afflicted with four strokes and a brain aneurysm.

On July 13, 2007, as I was boarding a flight from San Francisco following a speech, I received a call from Joe's brother, Tom

McDonough, telling me that Andrew was dying and that they did not expect him to make it through the night.

Landing late that evening in Philadelphia, I headed straight to the hospital, arriving after midnight. It was so quiet in the hospital that I thought I was too late. As I approached the room, I was intercepted by family. They told me that Andrew was still breathing but the end was near. We gathered around Andrew's bed and prayed that God would receive Andrew into heaven. At 1:55 PM on July 14, he passed away.

Following the funeral, Joe told me he planned to quit his banking job and start a foundation for childhood cancer in Andrew's name. I tried to discourage him from dropping his career to devote all his energy to such an endeavor. I thought I understood how hard it would be to keep on going with such a complicated project after the emotions and passion drain out and everyone had to move on with life. But Joe wanted to pay it forward and he felt it would help him to heal.

So before long, the Andrew McDonough B+ Foundation was formed. Andrew's blood type, B+, reflected the perfect message— "be positive" in the fight to survive and the fight against childhood cancer. Throughout his illness, Andrew inspired many others to be positive and understand their own blessings. Today, The B+ Foundation in honor of Andrew funds cutting-edge childhood cancer research and provides financial support to families of children with cancer nationwide. It also spreads the B+ message: "It's not a grade, it's an attitude."

I have counseled many amputees over the years. My personal experience as an amputee, combined with "peer visitor" training that I received at Walter Reed Hospital, has enabled me to help amputees with a road map of what to expect short and long term as they struggle with their new state in life. I am not a professional counselor, so any connections in this area have resulted from the fact that people know my story and reach out to me on a personal level. Keith Powell came to my attention one day as I was leaving the local YMCA after a workout. I was approached by Keith's wife, Luann, who was working at the "Y" as a part-time childcare assistant.

Luann introduced herself and asked if I might have a minute to speak with her. She was very nervous, and her words came out almost frantic as her eyes filled with tears. She explained that her husband, Keith, only thirty-eight years old, had just lost his leg below the knee from diabetes. He was very depressed, and she wanted to know if I would talk to him. I said sure, and we set up a brief meeting for the following week.

Keith Powell was a blue-collar guy, working as a carpenter by day and a bartender by night. Known as "Big Daddy," he checked in at about 6'0" and 190 lbs. on a muscular frame. We had a long talk covering the usual questions about "phantom pain," balance, prosthetics, and recovery time. The more I talked to Keith, the more I liked him. He was humble, long-suffering, religious, and last but certainly not least, a diehard Philadelphia Eagles fan.

Over the next couple of years Keith's diabetes got worse. His kidneys began to fail, and he was slowly losing his sight. Eventually, he needed dialysis and went completely blind, all the while hopeful that he could somehow stop the progress of the disease. Unfortunately, things only got worse, and he became what we might call my case of *Tuesdays with Morrie*, since we met every ten days or so to talk.

During my visits with him at his home, we talked mostly about sports. We covered the Eagles past and present including many adventures from my own Eagles past. He also loved to discuss his favorite TV show, *Investigative Discovery* with Sgt. Joe Kenda, to which we were both addicted.

Joe Kenda was a retired Colorado Springs homicide detective responsible for solving more than three hundred murders during his long and storied career. The re-creation of those "who done it" crimes with Kenda's dry wit and vengeful commentary were always intriguing and entertaining. Anytime he started unraveling a case and closed in on the killer, he would often make a declaration of, "my, my, my"—an expression Keith and I adopted frequently to make a point with each other.

Facing the amputation of his fingers, Keith asked me if I would accompany him to the hospital. I joined him that day and on two other occasions for the amputations. He eventually lost all eight fingers—one at a time. I was glad he could not see me tear up as they clipped each finger in a two-minute clip and sew procedure.

I thought I had been through a lot of pain and trauma in my life, but I have never seen a human being suffer as much as Keith. Yet, with the end coming, he was happier most days than half the people I have met in this life. For a while, I could not make sense of it until one day, he told me that he was mentally and spiritually at a peace. It was a peace that he said he had never experienced as the man known as "Big Daddy." He explained further that being at the mercy of other people to live allowed him to completely understand that God was in control. He would tell himself, *I can live with that.* And he did—better than most of us without his many crosses to bear.

A few months before he passed away, I went to visit him in dialysis where we were always one on one with our conversations. When he first heard my voice that day, he said, "Wow, Kevin, I was just thinking about us."

"You and me?" I asked.

"Hell, yes," he said. "I was just thinking that if God took all of the working parts of our bodies, he'd still be four fingers short. How about that?" We both laughed heartily.

After Keith died, I was privileged to deliver two eulogies in his honor. Looking back now, I must admit that what started out as me counseling him, ended with him mentoring to me on friendship, courage and true faith in God. My, my, my, "Big Daddy," you schooled us all!

Matt Szczur's story comes from a different angle but is no less astonishing. I met Matt through my association with Villanova football and coach Andy Talley. Andy started a bone marrow donor registry drive in 1992. During that first year, Talley and his team registered more than two hundred student athletes and coaches from the Villanova community. He hosted donor drives with his team until 2008 when he joined with the "Be the Match Registry." Also in 2008, Coach Talley expanded his efforts by forming a program called "Get in the Game, Save a Life" (GITG). The organization has enlisted over eighty other college football teams to participate in the bone marrow registry. Collectively, these schools have added over 83,000 names to the registry. Nearly four hundred patients have been given a second chance at life because of Talley's initiative. Here is one story that truly inspires:

In the fall of 2007, Matt Sczcur (pronounced "Caesar") entered Villanova accepting a scholarship to play football. He was also recruited to play baseball. After batting a rather lofty .681 during his senior year of high school, Matt was already being followed by major league baseball scouts. During his junior year in 2009, Matt was having an outstanding football season and was a leading candidate for the FCS Offensive Player of the Year. Just before the end of the regular season, with the playoffs set to begin, it was discovered that Matt was a donor match for a six-month-old baby girl in Ukraine named Anastasia Olkhovsky. Without hesitation, Matt was ready to give up the rest of the season to donate his bone marrow. Just days before the procedure was to be performed, however, Anastasia suffered a setback, and the extraction had to be postponed until early 2010.

Not only did Matt lead the Villanova squad to a national championship on December 18, but he finished with 270 all-purpose yards, scored two touchdowns, and was named the most valuable player of the game. Then, three months later, Matt interrupted his baseball season to undergo the grueling extraction of his bone marrow. Following the three-week long recovery from the effects of the procedure, he returned to the Villanova baseball team. In his first game back, on his first at-bat, he hit the first pitch out of the park for a home run.

A strict confidentiality policy keeps the bone marrow donor and recipient anonymous for at least a year following the procedure before any contact is allowed. On November 19, 2011, Matt and Anastasia's family were informed of each other's identities. A short time later, Matt, Anastasia, and her parents were connected via Skype and a translator. Anastasia's mother closed the call after a short conversation addressing Matt directly. "You are not a stranger, you are family," she said. "You saved my child's life. You breathed a part of your life into my daughter. The doctors helped you do this and God himself!"

As a Comcast's college football analyst that year, I had the opportunity to interview Matt Szczur about his outstanding season. It was prior to his bone marrow donation, so we covered that subject as well. During the interview, a very animated Matt mentioned that although the survival rate for the procedure was only sixty percent, he was certain that his recipient would make it through. When I asked him how he could be so confident he answered, "Because she'll have my blood!" It was not an egotistical or arrogant answer, but in my mind just a reflection of the positive attitude that winners so often have.

Matt Szczur signed with the Chicago Cubs in 2011 and earned a World Series ring before being traded to the San Diego Padres. On his first return visit to Wrigley Field in 2017, he threw out a Cubs' runner at home plate.

I have been an emcee for three of Andy Talley's fundraisers called "The Bash," and each has included the uniting of one of the recipients with their donor for the first time. One such encounter I especially remember involved a 6'3"and 275-pound lineman, John Stephens from Cortland State University.

When I met the little girl recipient and her mother on stage, she reached out without hesitation and embraced the big athlete standing next to me. It was almost as if the young man was a family member. He held her in his arms while her mother read an emotional thank you about how grateful she was for this gift of life. There wasn't a dry eye in the place.

Approximately ten years ago, I had the privilege of meeting retired Brigadier General Jon Reynolds. At a glance, there is nothing about Jon's appearance or demeanor that would provide a clue into his personal story. And the last person to tell you anything about what he has both endured and accomplished would be Jon Reynolds. I wanted to mention Jon's story because, unlike my own story of survival and recovery where I was surrounded by friends and family, Jon had to survive and battle back through long periods of isolation.

Growing up in suburban Philadelphia, Jon set his sights on becoming a fighter pilot. After graduation from Trinity College, he entered Air Force flight training. Soon flying the F-100 Super Sabre, Jon's squadron was deployed during the Cuban Missile Crisis loaded with nuclear weapons to be used if the Russian's launched a missile. In 1963, Jon was deployed to South Vietnam where he completed 165 missions in the L-19 Bird Dog as a forward air controller. Small, slow and vulnerable to enemy fire, "Bird Dog" pilots joked that their job was "to fly around until you get shot at, and then call in an air strike."

Jon returned to Vietnam in 1965, flying the F-105 "Thunderchief," attacking targets in North Vietnam. On November 28, 1965, he was shot down on his twenty-fifth mission sustaining a broken jaw and two broken shoulders while ejecting from the fast-moving fighter. Jon would endure inhumane treatment for much of his seven years as a POW, including solitary confinement and starvation. His leadership and resilience have been noted in books on the POW experience such as Alvin Townley's *Defiant* and Lee Ellis' *Leading with Honor: Leadership Lessons from the Hanoi Hilton.*

After being repatriated in 1973, Jon wasted no energy on regrets about the lost years of his life. He challenged himself in new ways and soon earned a PhD in history from Duke University and he went on to direct the air power and military history studies program at the U.S. Air Force Academy. From 1982 to 1988, Jon served as the United States' air and defense attaché to the People's Republic of China. Following his retirement from the Air Force in 1990, he returned to China as president of Raytheon China.

Recently, I had the opportunity to introduce Jon at the dinner following our "Dick Vermeil" golf event and the entire room rose and gave him a sustained ovation. The lifelong Philadelphia sports fan was being cheered by the very professional athletes he had cheered-on since he was a kid. It was great moment, recognizing a real Philly hero.

I have met and counseled several cancer patients over the years. Many of those individuals are still with us today, a testament to advances in treatment and their amazing positive attitudes. Unfortunately, any words of encouragement I could muster were of little use in the battle to save two of the most important people in my life: my sister Karen and the great Dr. Ralph Marcove.

Being the next sibling in line growing up, Karen and I always had a special relationship. In an odd sort of way, I always felt that I might have had a little something to do with Karen meeting her future husband. While playing in the North-South Shrine game in 1973, I spent some time with Glen Nardi. As the Naval Academy team captain playing for the South squad, I was encouraged to introduce myself to Glen by my friend Larry Pietropaulo. Larry was also at the Academy and a teammate of Glen's on the Middies Wrestling team. I last saw Glen at the airport as I was leaving Miami, and we parted saying we hoped to connect again in the future.

A couple of years later, in one of those "small world" experiences, I received a call from Karen, who at the time was serving in the Navy as a nurse. "Kevin," she said. "I'm dating an officer here who played football for Navy. He said he knows you and Larry. His name is Glen Nardi."

About a year later, Karen and Glen were married and would go on to have five children. Although Karen, Glen, and the kids lived in Greenville, South Carolina, we stayed in touch as much as possible. Tragically, Karen was diagnosed with ovarian cancer in 1998. Survival at that time from ovarian cancer was

My brothers and sisters with Karen
Megan, Kerry, Patty, Karen, Kevin and Sean

almost unheard of, but Karen was determined to put up a fight by limiting her pain medication so she could communicate with family to the very end. She fought to hang on to the point that family members had to tell her it was OK to let go. She died June 30, 2001 and was eulogized for her valiant fight against the unrelenting disease that took her. It was said, "She never complained of her situation because she accepted it as a cross from God."

Considered to be "out of the woods" after ten years following the amputation, I was nonetheless directed to return to Sloan Kettering at least once a year for a check-up. In the year 2000, I was twenty years out from my surgery when I made the annual trek. Having once dreaded these trips to Manhattan, I now looked forward to them because I would get to see the great Dr. Marcove, the man who saved my life. Not everyone can point to one person who actually saved his or her life, but I can assure you that for those who have had that experience, the bond is sealed forever.

As I sat in the waiting room that day and went through the preliminary steps prior to seeing the Doc, all appeared normal. And since Marcove's style could often seem abrupt or distracted, I did not realize at first that something was wrong. Maybe he was just in a bad mood, I thought. As we were wrapping up, he gave me the news. "Kevin, I will be turning your case over. I have pancreatic cancer and do not have long to live."

What a sad irony. The miracle worker who had saved so many, could not save himself. He died on January 9, 2001. His obituary in the *New York Times* provided some details on his many medical accomplishments in the field of orthopedic oncology. To my surprise, it noted that he was an accomplished drummer and a recognized authority in the field of Asian art. It also stated that he had authored books and more than three hundred articles on bone tumors. It concluded, "Dr. Marcove was dedicated to the treatment and care of bone tumors and gave a special gift to the people whose lives he touched."

CHAPTER 27

||||||||||||||||||||||||||||||||||||||||||||||||||||||||||||||||||||||||||||||||||||||

Walter Reed and the Amputee Ward

"How many of you here today are Dallas Cowboy fans?"

After 10:00 PM on a summer night in 2005, I was watching a Phillies game into the late innings when my phone rang. It was my friend John Riley, "KR, sorry to bother you so late but figured you would be watching the Phillies. Quick, turn on channel 12. I want you to see something." Click.

For the next half-an-hour, I was riveted to my television watching a documentary about the amputation ward at the Walter Reed Army Hospital. When it was over. I called John back. "John," I said. "I should go down there, I think I can help."

John replied, "I know, I'll call Senator Carper and see if he can set up a visit."

The rest of this chapter was contributed by John Riley

By 2005, I had known Kevin Reilly for approximately thirty years. Along with our friend Dave Jenkins and our wives, I had dinner with him the night before he left for Sloan Kettering for the operation that would remove nearly twenty percent of his body and save his life.

At that time, we knew there was a strong possibility he might not survive the surgery, or that the famous Dr. Marcove might not be able to extract all the desmoid disease. Following Kevin's recovery, we continued to work together at Xerox, co-chaired a highly successful charity golf tournament, and managed the professional boxing career of former national amateur heavyweight champion Henry Milligan. We rarely went through a day without speaking to each other.

During our time together, I had watched Kevin counsel people with addictions, amputations, and fatal diseases. A man of deep faith, he seemed to have a gift for saying the right thing in the most difficult of circumstances. So, the night I happened to come across the Walter Reed documentary while channel surfing, I knew immediately there was another mission for my friend.

More than a year following the invasion of Iraq in 2003, our troops were targeted by terrorists and insurgents using improvised explosive devices (IEDs). Typically made from artillery shells and other high explosive ordnance, IEDs would be responsible for as many as half the deaths suffered by U.S. and coalition forces in both Iraq and Afghanistan. Due to protective body armor and the advanced lifesaving efforts of the modern military, many soldiers who in previous wars might not have survived now made it through, but often with the loss of one or more limbs. The first stop in the U.S. for most of these amputation cases was Walter Reed, either for additional surgery or for initial therapy.

I had told Kevin I would take the lead to line up a visit. Working through Senator Tom Carper of Delaware and his staff, I soon learned that not just anyone was cleared to visit with these recovering wounded warriors. When we finally got to the right person at Walter Reed, they were cautious if not skeptical about volunteers who wanted to speak to the patients. Also, there seemed to be a steady parade of celebrities, politicians and assorted dignitaries who visited the hospital, so just managing the flow was a challenge.

Finally, following a phone interview with the officer in charge of the amputation ward, Captain Katie, Kevin, and his special assistant, yours truly, were cleared for the mission in October 2005. Not that Kevin needed additional inspiration for his visit that day, but I suggested we head to Washington early and visit some of the nation's monuments, including the recently dedicated World War II memorial.

When we arrived at the hospital, we were escorted by Captain Katie and met some of the doctors. We were both counseled on the physical and mental condition of the patients. Some had arrived within the last forty-eight hours and were being prepped for further surgery, some were recovering from wounds and surgery and others had been fitted for prosthesis and were being readied for discharge. They then told us that doctors and staff wanted to sit in on Kevin's talk. I wasn't sure whether they wanted to hear him speak or ensure that neither one of us stepped out of line.

As approximately twenty patients in beds or wheelchairs and another dozen doctors and nurses gathered, I thought that this was the toughest audience I had ever seen. Many of the amputees still had blood on their bandages. Some were clearly in pain, and there wasn't a smile in the room. I must admit that I was very uncomfortable at the sight of a couple of women amputees. This was not the Army I had been a part of thirty-five years ago. As I was taking it all in, glad that I was not the one that had to address the group, Kevin turned to me. "How about you introduce me," he said. For a second, my mind went totally blank, my throat dry and I was groping to remember what team the former Philadelphia Eagle had played for. Somehow, I managed to stumble through it and then stepped out of the way.

Despite all our prep and travel, Kevin never mentioned exactly how he was going to approach this extraordinary speaking event. I was a bit taken back by his opening: "How many of you here today are Dallas Cowboy fans?" A couple of hands went half way up. "Well then, I will speak slowly for you Dallas fans." A couple amputees managed a half smile and Kevin went on to share his personal story. You could see the audience's mood change. They were hearing from someone who had suffered a traumatic loss to his body like them, as well as the loss of his career and athletic dreams. But there he was, tall and strong with some life instructions on how they could make it too. They were hanging on his every word, smiling, nodding agreement, and soon sitting higher on their beds and wheelchairs.

One of the favorite moments in Kevin's personal story is how he was told by a well-meaning volunteer at Sloan Kettering to buy himself clip-on ties because he would never be able to tie his tie again. Of course, Kevin not only learned to tie his tie one-handed, he began to use the story in his motivational speeches. Towards the end of his talk, Kevin told the rapt audience, "Don't let anyone tell you what you can't do. Don't let others put limitations on you." At that moment, he took off his tie and within seconds, tied it back on, pulling it tight into a perfect knot.

The room exploded with shouts and cheers from these wounded warriors. If there was another desert to cross or hill to take, they would have been on their way. I could not see through the tears streaming down my face and I thought to myself: *This is exactly the reason God put this man on earth—just for this very moment.*

Kevin closed out his talk and lingered for over an hour speaking with each soldier individually. He told me afterwards that they wanted to ask questions about some of their most intimate fears, everything from how their spouses and children would react to them to how he dealt with the phantom pain they were already experiencing.

As we were leaving, Captain Katie asked Kevin if he would be willing to become what they called a "peer visitor," a position that involved a couple of days of training. For the next few years Kevin would make several trips back to Water Reed to counsel amputees.

As we were leaving the hospital that day, I mentioned that I never met an Army officer as attractive as Captain Katie. Kevin, who was single at the time replied, "Yes, but she had a ring on!"

CHAPTER 28

‖‖

Accepting My Condition

"Hey mister, what happened to your arm?"

O nce I was able to accept my new appearance and limitations, my attitude following surgery became extremely positive. I felt lucky to be alive, back to work and with family, and able to exercise without pain. I decided to reset my life and not look back. Football was gone, but in most other things, I expected to compete with the same dedication I had before. I made it a point of pride that I would accept no adjustments by society to my condition, even though I had to do some personal adjusting.

The first major change I had to make was to accept the fact that everything took longer, including the simple things I took for granted in the past such as getting ready for work in the morning. I was blessed to be supported by family and friends during the initial months. In my later years, following the divorce, I lived extensively on my own, but in those early days following the amputation, it would have been far more challenging without the help.

The fact is you take for granted the things you were born with, like two arms, hands, and shoulders. Naturally, I missed some of the simplest things that I could no longer do until it was taken away, such as a big bear hug, hitting a pitched baseball, playing guitar, or even bench-pressing or shooting pool. I found there was an extensive list of things you cannot do with one arm, or at least with any satisfaction.

Maybe it was my faith or my competitive background coming out, but I decided I would not dwell on these things. It was wasted energy to spend time feeling sorry for myself. There were constant reminders in the everyday lives of people who faced far greater challenges than me. This lesson was especially driven home during my time counseling amputees at Walter Reed and working with families dealing with cancer or serious addictions.

I have probably overlooked a few limitations that bothered me in the early days, but I am proud to say there are some things that normally require two arms or hands that I managed to adjust to. For instance, I can now tie a necktie, tie my shoelaces, swim (or at least stay afloat and move forward), drive a car, put up Christmas lights (better than Clark Griswold from the movie *Christmas Vacation*), chop firewood, drive a nail and use most power tools, cut my grass, paint, and play golf.
(I am not the first amputee to relearn how to play golf after losing an arm, but I may be the first who actually improved using only one arm!) Most importantly, I'm pretty good at "babysitting" the grandkids—my favorite one-armed activity.

It was not always easy, but repetition and patience carried me through. As I climbed these little daily mountains, I also discovered that my new reality brought new challenges. Some were subtle, some were not, and others would stay with me for the rest of my life.

Two of the biggest issues I have dealt with have been that I am easily recognized with one arm and I receive an abundance of stares as I go through everyday life. The recognition is generally a positive. Someone only has to catch a glimpse of me out of the corner of their eye and they are yelling hello from a block away.

A funny story along these lines occurred in a San Francisco hotel restaurant. In January of 1985, Cathy and I were in town on a sales recognition trip to attend Super Bowl XIX. Entering the restaurant one night with a group of Xerox managers from around the country, we immediately noticed a lot of excitement in the room because Joe DiMaggio was having dinner there. Joe was well-known to nearly everyone at the time due to his Hall of Fame baseball career with the Yankees and because he had been married to sex symbol Marilyn Monroe. To most of the ladies present, though, who were unaware of his fifty-six-game hitting streak, Joe was simply a famous line in the hit Simon and Garfunkel song *Mrs. Robinson* or as the TV pitchman, "Mr. Coffee."

A small crowd was gathered around DiMaggio seeking autographs. Based on my experience with Joe on his visits to Wilmington, I knew he was notoriously shy, which some mistook as rude. I crossed the room with Cathy and several others, hoping he might recognize me—if not by the face, by the missing arm. Apparently, relieved to see someone he knew, Joe immediately called out my name and invited us to join his table. We sat with him for the next forty-five minutes while one Xerox executive after another came up to see if they could meet one of America's iconic figures.

While sitting with Joe, he became interested in the Super Bowl pins that were on my hat. Collecting and trading pins was an ongoing game of sorts during the Super Bowl–week activities. Total strangers with hats of their own would stop you and try to make a trade with maybe a double that they had or another pin deemed to be rare. Some pins were considered more valuable than others.

I would liken it to trading baseball cards in the '50s and '60s. Joe traded me for a Xerox pin, and I promised him that I would supply him with more of them the following day. Sure enough, he sought me out the next day to get those pins. As he walked away, he had a smile on his face like a kid who had just traded for two Joe DiMaggio rookie baseball cards. Go figure!

Joe DiMaggio

The encounter with DiMaggio seemed to take on a life greater than Super Bowl XIX and the one-arm man got to bask in the glow for days afterwards.

At times, the stares I receive are a little unsettling, but they have led to several interesting encounters and maybe even a few lessons. The most obvious and penetrating stares I receive are from children, especially younger kids between two and five years old. I may have known them since birth, but one day around that age, they react as if my arm disappeared in the middle of the night.

I do not know the reason for their sudden awareness, but it has happened to me many times with children, including each of my ten grandchildren, as well as my nieces and nephews, and the kids of friends and neighbors. I can see it coming. First, they suddenly look at me with a confused look on their face and focus directly at my empty sleeve. After a short delay and with a look of astonishment, they ask, "Hey, Pop Pop (or Uncle Kev or Mr. Reilly), what happened to your arm?"

They might ask in disbelief, amazement, or curiosity, but mostly I hear them ask with sympathy, "Are you OK?" Up until that point in their young lives, most of them have never witnessed a person with one arm, and they are not able to come to terms with what they are seeing.

It happens to me the most often at a grocery or department store. I'll be wandering down an aisle when a child will spot me, walk away from their parent and come up to say, "Hey, mister, what happened to your arm?" Their embarrassed parent will look for the next hole to climb into.

At first, I struggled a bit to respond but soon learned to enjoy these exchanges. A child psychologist friend gave me some valuable insight into how kids perceive such a physical loss. Their limited experience in this area is based on losing teeth that grow back, broken bones that mend, and cuts and bruises that heal and go away. At this age, getting into any type of explanation about amputation would go right over their heads. And really, they just want to be assured that everything will be OK.

So, on the advice of my psychologist friend, I follow this routine: I stoop down to their eye level and tell them that I had a bad "boo-boo" on my arm but the doctor took the boo-boo away with my arm to make me better. Now, I'm all healed and everything is going to be fine.

I might get a follow-up question along the lines of, "Will it grow back?" As much as I would like to laugh, I tell them, "Maybe, you never know." I was told that any other answer was a slippery slope that led to an extra interrogation. Most children accept my explanation and are satisfied with my answer. I always smile at the parent or person that the child is with and give them a wave or response to show I am not at all bothered by the situation.

There have been a few funny stories over the years. My grandson Andrew, at about age two-and-a-half, did not take my answer too well and wanted to dive deeper. He asked if he could see under my shoulder prosthetic to get the real story. I removed my prosthetic and revealed some rather serious and pronounced scars from my operation. His eyes grew large and he recoiled from my chest.

"Andrew, it's all right," I told him. "These boo boos are all better now and they don't hurt at all." He was still absolutely stunned, so I asked him, "Are you OK, buddy?"

Andrew replied, "Yeah, Pop Pop, but don't ask me to kiss that boo boo!"

The second time I vividly remember was my grandnephew and technical wizard Jack Sutton, who, after a few months of my canned explanation, came up to me with a potential solution. "Uncle Kev, I think if you hold your nose and close your mouth real tight and blow as hard as you can, your arm might pop back out of your shoulder!"

Another recent funny incident occurred when I was asked to speak to my grandson's kindergarten class. To get the arm issue out of the way early, I asked the kids gathered around me what was different about me. A little girl raised her hand and I called on her. She said shyly, "Mister, you are old!" That was a first, but she had a point—I had recently joined the Medicare ranks!

Staring children, I have no problem dealing with, but adults are sometimes a different story. I love to walk or run on the beach in Stone Harbor, New Jersey. I do it for exercise and head at least a mile up the beach and back in just a swimsuit. My four-quarter amputation leaves a very large void on my left side, which is impossible not to notice. So, the stares begin.

I realize that staring at my condition is natural and a built-in mental cue that "something is not right here." I have come to anticipate and identify a few of the categories of stares I have run into over the years. Here are some of my favorites:

The Sneaky Stare: A quick glance and an even quicker look away, as if to say, "I didn't see anything."

The Over-the-Shoulder Stare: After passing me, they turn around for a longer look. I can feel it on the back of my head!

The Sunglass Stare: "He doesn't know I'm staring at him through my sunglasses, does he?"

The Poor Soul Stare: "This poor guy's life must be a disaster!"

The Stare with Hand Salute: Not common, but it is a nod from that person believing I am a wounded veteran who lost an arm in combat.

If you happen to be in a predicament like mine, I suggest when you realize someone is staring at you, acknowledge them and give them a cordial greeting. A simple smile can work just as well.

One nice thing I have noticed, even with children, has been that very shortly after their initial encounter with me, they adapt and accept. When I coached my children's teams, by the second practice the kids no longer noticed I was different. At work and among family and friends it can often be a subject to have some fun with. My son Brett did an impersonation of me at my sixtieth birthday party that brought the house down.

In my thirty-eight years as an amputee, I have had very few negative experiences. I think this is an incredible affirmation of the human spirit and how most people have good hearts and souls. One of those negative encounters is one of my favorite stories.

My first wife, Cathy, and I were on vacation in Hawaii. As we sat on the famous Waikiki Beach in Honolulu, I got up from my chair and went into a beachfront convenience store located about a hundred feet away to buy us a drink. Two loud and obnoxious drunks saddled up behind me. Because they were so high, they were talking louder than they realized.

"Look at the gimp in front of us," one of them said to his friend as they giggled.

"He must swim in circles," the other laughed.

Then one of them said to me, "Hey man, what happened to your arm and shoulder?"

I turned around ever so slowly and deadpanned, "Shark, ten years ago. Right here on this beach. My wife and I are celebrating the ten-year anniversary of the event."

Their mouths were wide open. "No way, man," one of them responded. "For real … for real!?"

I told them, "Of course. I'd never kid about that," and left the store.

Cathy and I noticed them from our spot on the beach the next couple of days, and they stayed clear of the water.

CHAPTER 29

||||||||||||||||||||||||||||||||||||||||||||||||||||||||||||||||||||||||||||||||||||||||||||

My Life Today

"Nobody cares how much you know, until they know about how much you care!"

After getting divorced in August of 1997, I began to date for the first time in more than twenty years. I learned quickly that the landscape had changed rather dramatically. In this world, I was a rookie again. Dating websites were taking center stage, and I also had to learn how to navigate in the emerging world of social media.

I dated on and off for about a dozen years, and met some very nice people—but not the perfect someone I hoped to spend the rest of my life with. At one point, several years into my search, my good friend Father Richard Dililio, an Oblate priest who taught during my time at Salesianum, joked to me, "Don't forget the Oblates … three hots and a cot. It's not a bad life." I believe he was joking—then again, who knows?

Just when I had almost given up on my quest to find, "Miss Right," it happened—almost like in the movies!

On a beautiful August afternoon in Stone Harbor, I had just arrived for the weekend and decided to walk up the beach to see if I could find my sisters. Megan, Kerry, and my parents all had places in town, and they liked to relax at a spot on 90th Street, about ten blocks up from my condo. I soon found them having lunch with their friend Lena Salus, whom I knew, and Paula McDermott, whom I would meet for the first time.

From the moment Paula smiled and said, "Glad to meet you," I was intrigued. I pulled up a chair right next to her and we began to chat. Speaking to this beautiful, charming woman I did not know where the time went. I learned that she was vice president of marketing for WPVI-TV in Philadelphia, the local ABC station. Coincidentally, I was scheduled the following week to assume my play-by-play duties for the Eagles pre-season games, which would be carried by ABC. Paula had a role in marketing and advertising for the games.

I don't know where the next couple hours went, but when I looked up both my sisters and Lena had smiles on their faces like the Cheshire cat. Paula and Lena went home that evening, but for the next several days I continued to think about her and soon decided to give her a call. We set a weekday lunch date, and over the two hours, it was clear that the magic continued. We covered a lot of ground that day, discussing where we stood as single people and nothing she said discouraged me in the least. When I walked Paula to her car after lunch, we embraced. From that first kiss, I knew she was the one. We began to see each other regularly and were quickly in love.

It was convenient that Paula was already friends with my three sisters, and it took no time for her to win over my adult children, grandchildren, and all my friends. A divorcée, Paula and her two sons, Davis, age twelve, and Matt, fourteen, lived in Wilmington, only three doors down from my sister Kerry. In less than a year we were engaged and planned to get married as soon as the 2011 football season ended. We might have moved more quickly, but Eagles broadcasts and other area high school and college games had me tied up every weekend.

Over Thanksgiving that year, as we started to focus on a date for the wedding, we discovered a problem: Where would we draw the line on what friends to invite? At this stage of our lives we both had large extended families and many great friends and business associates. That was when Paula said, "I have an idea. Why don't we get married in Las Vegas in February, when we plan to visit with your friend Larry Pietropaulo and his fiancée, Megan." At first, I thought she was joking … but hoped she wasn't. After a brief discussion, we concluded this would be the best way to avoid hurting anyone's feelings and then sealed the deal with an agreement that we would put all the money we saved on a large wedding into our new home.

Before Paula could change her mind, I placed a call to my friend Larry and asked if he and Megan would be our witnesses. So, on February 18, 2012, Paula and I were married in the original Las Vegas chapel. We had a great honeymoon weekend together, and we returned home ready and anxious to start our new lives together.

Kevin and Paula
Wedding Night 2012

Paula and I recently celebrated our fifth wedding anniversary. She is the love of my life and has helped me improve as a person to a level I believe I would never have reached on my own. I have also thoroughly enjoyed my relationship with her sons, who attended my alma mater, Salesianum before moving on to college. I know I am a lucky man to have found Paula and together we are experiencing the best years of our lives.

In addition to my good fortune in marriage, other recent milestones were my retirement from Xerox in 2006 and the Eagles broadcast team in 2016. These are major changes, yet somehow, I am busier than ever. On the broadcast front, I agreed to continue my association with Villanova and Salesianum football, plus key regional high school games for Comcast SportsNet. I love staying connected to my alma maters and thoroughly enjoy maintaining my contact with the great people at these institutions, including coaches and students. It was great fun at Villanova, being up close and personal as my friend, basketball coach Jay Wright led his Wildcat squad to the NCAA Championship in 2016.

Another activity that occupies a lot of my time has been running the annual Dick Vermeil Boy Scouts' Golf Tournament. Held every June, this event is a great excuse to remain in contact with my old and new Eagle football friends as well as coaching legend Dick Vermeil. Still going strong at eighty, "Coach" runs a very successful wine business and is in demand as a public speaker. Vermeil is often kidded about his emotional tendencies, including tearing up at public events. All I can say is, this is the real Vermeil. He has a huge heart and such a deep affection for so many people that he has probably lost count. His most famous saying fits him perfectly: "Nobody cares how much you know, until they know about how much you care!"

Another labor of love for me is my work with the Desmoid Tumor Research Foundation. I have served in a couple capacities with the organization including chairing their annual fundraiser, "Running for Answers." This is an annual 5k race, held in

Dick Vermeil Golf Tournament 2016, Kevin Sweet, Kevin, Steve Kupcha, Navy SEAL Ret., Dick Vermeil, and BG Jon Reynolds, USAF Ret.

Philadelphia in conjunction with a medical seminar that I have had the opportunity to address. These events give much needed exposure to a disease that almost no one had heard of when my tumor was discovered in the late '70s. Like so many forms of cancer, the key to success is research and early detection. My hope is that through this book, thousands more will come to know what desmoid is.

While I have certainly had my challenges over the past forty years, I would not trade my life with anyone. My three wonderful kids grew up, married great spouses, and produced ten incredible grandkids. As of this writing, they range in age from four to sixteen. Rarely a day goes by that I am not in contact with at least one of them. In fact, I have become the default babysitter and cheerleader, often dropping everything to fill in at the last minute or attend that all important T-ball game.

While I have enjoyed separate careers in professional football, sales, marketing, broadcasting, and even a year as a sports agent, my continuing professional endeavor remains my public speaking. From my time addressing football fans and kids' sports teams as an NFL rookie, to my current role as a motivational speaker, my time in front of an audience is my chance to have an impact on people.

I find myself these days speaking to more and more corporate meetings, which gives me an opportunity to discuss leadership. We often debate if leaders are born or if leaders are made. In my own experience, I did not always seek leadership, but sometimes it just hits you in the face and you must rise to the occasion—or get out of the way.

This was the case for me in my senior year of high school, when I was elected captain of both the football and basketball teams. With some guidance from coaches and other important people in my life, I realized that my conduct and the example I set were far more important than any words I might say. These sports leadership roles would continue into college, when I was elected co-captain of the Villanova football team, and the pros, where I became captain of special teams for the Eagles and assistant player representative to the NFL Players' Association. I have also served in various leadership positions during my business career and while serving on non-profit boards.

In my speeches, I focus on the great leaders with whom I have worked, as well as the principles and style that they embody and that I strive to emulate. From my football experience, the two most outstanding leaders I have observed are Super Bowl-winning coaches Dick Vermeil and Don Shula. But, I emphasize that one does not have to be a renowned Super Bowl coach or run a large organization to grasp the

With Vermeil

principles of good leadership. My parents and my high school athletic director, Father Ashenbrenner, were probably the three most influential leaders I knew in my early life. They had no formal leadership training, but as products of the Great Depression and World War II, they developed an ability to gain the willing and enthusiastic support of others to get a job done well. They lived by example my favorite leadership quote from basketball coach Don Meyer, "Good leaders are demanding without being demeaning."

Wherever I am in the country, people approach me after my talks. Sometimes, it is an old friend I have not seen in decades or a football fan who connected with a story I shared, but most of the time it is someone who is dealing with their own challenge in life, looking for a word of encouragement or some guidance on where to go for help. This is a role that I truly love—maybe not as perfect as being a grandfather, but still pretty good.

EPILOGUE

"Tough times don't last, but tough people do."

While all of us can relate to the value in our lives of family and friends, I recognize that the definition and significance of faith and fortitude can vary greatly from one individual to another. My own faith, from my early days in Catholic school to my role as a lector today, has varied in intensity over the years— rising to a fever pitch in the hours before my surgery. But even in my rather raucous years in the NFL, I always found support and solace through moments of prayer and introspection. To me, it was as if I always had someone's support behind me; someone to turn to in time of need. It was perhaps a bit silly that I tried to use that hidden power to get a hit in a baseball game or a win over Middletown or Dallas, but it sure came in handy when I was facing surgery and recovering from divorce.

My talks over the years primarily focus on how fortitude helped to power me through what seemed at times to be mountains of adversity. Clearly, others have faced greater challenges than me during their lives, but not everyone has a platform—an opportunity to share their story with others.

One question I routinely receive after a speech is if I have written a book about my life. People say they want to share my story with a family member or friend in the hope that it might inspire them to face the demon in their lives. It is a humbling experience to think you may be able to help another human being through the example of your own life, as imperfect at as I know mine to be.

But I know that people like my sister Karen, Keith Powell, Jon Reynolds, and Matt Sczcur have inspired me to push on when the going gets tough. One of my favorite expressions is, "Tough times don't last, but tough people do."

I mentioned in the beginning of the book that various elements of my upbringing helped to prepare me to push on when I could have given up. At the top of the list stands my mother and father, both fine examples of the Greatest Generation. Even today, at ages eighty-seven and ninety-one respectively, they run a small business with the same enthusiasm they used to root me on as a Philadelphia Eagle.

The institution of Salesianum helped to lay the groundwork for my athletic endeavors, but more importantly, it instilled some of the values of the "Gentleman Saint" that I hope I continue to carry with me in life. The school's motto, *Tenui Nec Dimittan* ("I have taken

John and Kevin with Rear Admiral Tim Szymanski

hold and will not let go"), is imprinted on my heart and soul. To me, it also means, "never give up." That one phrase, uttered quietly to myself over the years has helped get me through a thousand challenges both large and small.

For many years, I served on the board of Salesianum, and one of my proudest moments was to be inducted into their Hall of Fame in 2006, next to legends of the school such as Navy SEAL commander Tim Szymanski, National Guard Lt. General Frank Vavala, and coaches like Dim Montero and Father James "Buzz" O'Neill.

In April 2017, I had the honor of introducing Rear Admiral Szymanski at the annual Salesianum sports banquet. As we were leaving the reception to head into the dinner, the special operations warrior stopped the school principal, Father Beretta, to ask for a blessing.

Standing there next to him, I tried to comprehend some of the danger this valiant leader had faced on SEAL missions over his decades in service to our country. No doubt, his time at Salesianum had helped to provide a foundation to meet some of the challenges he would face in the years ahead. In his remarks to the students that night, he talked about Salesianum values like loyalty, discipline, and a thirst for knowledge, and to be prepared for adversity and for failures. I know that message resonated with me, and it seemed to strike a chord with the students and the sell-out crowd.

Looking back on my life and remembering that mind-numbing moment when Dr. Marcove said, "Kevin, you have a desmoid tumor and we will be lucky if I can save your arm." The pain, suffering and struggle to get through the operation and that first full year of recovery was really a blessing in disguise. It taught me that the human spirit was stronger than anything that could happen to me. It made me a survivor; it drove me to work harder and prepared me to face and overcome other obstacles in my life. And, most importantly, it gave me added empathy for others who were undergoing great life challenges and instilled in me a desire to provide support whenever I could.

Faith, Family, Friends, and Fortitude—if you have these four pillars in your life, you can survive and overcome a great deal. Take hold and never let go!

Mom Kay, Kevin, Son Brett, and Dad Francis X

Three beautiful women in my life -
daughter Brie, mom, and daughter Erin

Jake, Liam, Parker, Bowe, Roman, Georgie, Mae, Ruby, Sammy, and Andrew

Speaking at a banquet with Villanova basketball coach and friend Jay Wright

At a Villanova alumni function with good friend and Hall of Famer Howie Long

Kevin with Miami Super Bowl Kicker Garo Yepremain

1974 poster and People magazine centerfold

2016 Dick Vermeil Celebrity Golf Tournament